The 30-

How to Build Intimacy,

Day

Enhance Your Sex Life, and Strengthen

Sex

Your Relationship in **ONE MONTH'S TIME**

solution

VICTORIA ZDROK WILSON, JD, PhD and **JOHN WILSON, MFT**

A adamsmedia

Avon, Massachusetts

Published by
Adams Media, a division of F+W Media, Inc.
57 Littlefield Street, Avon, MA 02322. U.S.A.
www.adamsmedia.com

ISBN 10: 1-60550-680-X
ISBN 13: 978-1-60550-680-7
eISBN 10: 1-4405-2559-5
eISBN 13: 978-1-4405-2559-9

Printed in the United States of America.

10   9   8   7   6   5   4   3   2   1

Library of Congress Cataloging-in-Publication Data

Wilson, Victoria Zdrok.
The 30-day sex solution / Victoria Zdrok Wilson and John Wilson.
p. cm.
Includes bibliographical references and index.
ISBN-13: 978-1-60550-680-7 (alk. paper)
ISBN-13: 978-1-4405-2559-9 (ebk)
ISBN-10: 1-60550-680-X (alk. paper)
ISBN-10: 1-4405-2559-5 (ebk)
1. Sex. 2. Intimacy (Psychology) 3. Man-woman relationships. I. Wilson, John.
II. Title.
HQ31.W7732 2011
613.9'6—dc22
2011006234

This book is available at quantity discounts for bulk purchases.
For information, please call 1-800-289-0963.

Dedication

This book is dedicated to our parents, children, and patients who provide us with spiritual support, cognitive challenges, and infinite inspiration.

Contents

Introduction

A new epidemic is sweeping through America—a stultifying sexual stagnation that eats away at our libidos, extinguishes our passion for each other, and erects emotional walls between us.

Statistics show that as many as 17 million married people in the United States have no sex at all. Many of those who continue to have sex view it as boring, unsatisfying, and devoid of passion and romance. One study found that 25 percent of women are unable to achieve orgasm, 30 percent of women lack interest in sex, more than 30 percent of men suffer from premature ejaculation, and a high percentage of both men and women complain that they don't have sex often enough. Why do so many relationships turn sexless and unsatisfying? Sexual ennui (along with fatigue, work stress, children, aging, and marital conflict) lowers libido and insidiously destroys our passion for each other.

Our lifestyles provide fertile ground for the sexual-stagnation virus. Americans are an overworked, underslept, and overspent nation. The result? We tune out our partners. Because we are more distracted, distant, and aloof and less emotionally connected with each other than ever before, we experience less passion and sexual romance. Yet sexual passion is crucial to marital satisfaction; it's the cornerstone of a couple's happiness and a solid predictor of relationship longevity.

WHY YOU NEED THIS BOOK

You have probably opened this book because you wistfully miss the days of earth-shattering sexual coupling you used to have with your partner; because you secretly wish for more passion, romance, and a spark in your life; or because you wonder if there is more to sex than what you have experienced so far.

Although our culture promotes the blissful ideal of an eternal "happily ever after" as romance, the reality is that monogamy often brings monotony and "hastily ever after." As a couple who have been together for almost fifteen years, we, too, have struggled with growing boredom, diminished desire, and lack of time brought on by dual careers, ailing parents, and two challenging children. Despite being in the mental health field and treating couples on a regular basis, we managed to ignore our own relationship, succumbing to the very virus we strived to remedy in others.

THE SEX RX PROGRAM

Fortunately, we were able to recognize the waning of our passion for each other and to develop a program that has worked for us and for our patients. We call it Sex Rx. This thirty-day prescription includes physical and mental exercises and challenges to revive your passion and renew romance and desire in your sex life.

You may be surprised to find that our program focuses more on the mental exercises than on the physical ones. That's because we believe the brain is the most sensitive sexual organ. Although the right type and amount of physical friction are necessary to produce an orgasm, your mind is what gives meaning to the rush of pleasure you experience before, during, and after orgasm. When you remove negative emotional barriers, when you feel safe and connected to your partner, when your needs and fantasies are acknowledged and fulfilled, sex becomes more than a mere muscular twitch or a release of built-up tension.

That's why our program deals in depth with freeing your feelings and exploring your fantasies, and only briefly addresses some sexual positions and techniques. You can always find out about the right type of suggested physical friction in the innumerable sex manuals available on the market. Our program ambitiously aims to help you achieve thrilling, intimacy-building, soul-fulfilling sex through "sexercising" your mind.

Sex Rx Rule: Fantastic Sex = Feelings Freed + Fantasy Fulfilled + Friction Focused on Partner's Pleasure

HOW TO USE THE PROGRAM

If you're like most couples in committed relationships, you thought of sex as a special wedding present when you first got together. It was shiny and new, packaged beautifully in an alluring container, with a bow and gift note inscribed, "Your Passionate Hereafter." But when you unwrapped the fancy packaging and opened the box, to your dismay you discovered a complicated contraption consisting of countless parts with no assembly instructions or tools necessary to put it all together. It involved the elements of the past and the present, the self and the other, merger and separateness, personalization and objectification.

Parts of it worked, so you contented yourself with them, for now. To put the structure together required time and joint effort, and you probably intended to work on it but got distracted by work and family pressures. And so you shoved the box in the closet, leaving only the main mechanism, which seemed to work just fine.

Until it stopped working just fine. Then you remembered that you never bothered to put together the rest of the structure. That's what this book is for: to help you put it all together.

Although the aim of our program is to give you the tools necessary to assemble your sexual satisfaction structure, we cannot give you the exact assembly instructions—each individual has a unique blueprint of desire. It will be up to you to use these tools in the way that gives you the most sexual satisfaction.

Putting these pieces together will feel like hard work, because indeed it is. Relationships are infinitely complicated and challenging, even for the most savvy relationship experts. Our human nature makes it hard for us to be close and loving to one another all the time. We tend to hold on to negative memories, to exaggerate, internalize, and catastrophize. This makes it easy to blame and hard to let go, easy to brood and hard to be cheerful, easy to coexist and hard to stay genuinely connected.

But if you put in the effort required, you'll discover that relating to each other and staying passionate will become easier as you go along, and it will no longer feel like you're biking up a steep hill. You'll get a second wind, encouraged by the changes in yourself and your relationship. In addition to helping you with existing issues, our program is designed to help prevent future relationship problems. So stick with it, even when it seems challenging and tedious, even when you don't seem to see the desired change and you feel like giving up. A satisfying relationship is the most important predictor of success and happiness in life, and a goal worth the hard work it entails.

THE FIVE PARTS OF THE PROGRAM

This book consists of five main parts, or factors. Each of these factors is necessary to create and maintain passion in a long-term relationship.

1. **The Priority Factor:** If you don't prioritize your sex life, it will be last on your list, gathering dust somewhere on the back shelf of your multitasking brain. Making it a priority will affirm your dedicated commitment to the happiness of your relationship.

2. **The Intimacy Factor:** Intimacy is another crucial component of passion. In long-term relationships you have to know and like each other in order to want to have sex. Nothing puts a damper on passion faster than unresolved conflicts and negative feelings brought about by poor communication.

3. **The Novelty Factor:** Without novelty, a monogamous sex life quickly becomes monotonous, dreary, boring, and unsatisfying as you robotically go through the same motions.

4. **The Naughtiness Factor:** The naughtiness factor puts an extra zing in your passion as you sample formerly forbidden fruit.

5. **The Loftiness Factor:** Finally, elevating sex to a spiritual quest brings about unexpected heights of ecstasy.

Each part contains three chapters, and each chapter covers two days of this thirty-day program. Each day prescribes exercises to do that day.

STAYING ON TRACK

You may have days when you won't have time to do all the prescribed exercises, days you will slack off, days when your partner won't cooperate, days when you don't like some of the exercises or ideas, and days when other priorities may trump the program. That's to be expected. But don't give up if you get behind or if your partner is not putting in the same effort as you are. You can never force change upon your partner. You can only change yourself—but that change alone will be significant. It will improve your relationship and encourage your partner to change as well.

If you wish to become more passionate or to regain the desire you once had for each other, you first need to spend more time together as a couple. Spend this time on nonsexual activities that generate a sense of bonding, goodwill, and trust. Doing this will strengthen and deepen your relationship and allow the sexual activities in the program to take place in a relationship that is as intimate outside the bedroom as it is inside.

For the first two weeks of the program, you abstain from having intercourse with each other and instead focus on connecting mentally and emotionally. This will build up sexual excitement and anticipation while you are working on improving your libido, clearing your mind of sexual impediments, and changing your sexual script.

Ultimately, this program will spark your sexual self-actualization and sexual growth by encouraging you to begin a passionate journey of greater intimacy, physical health, emotional healing, intellectual stimulation, erotic exploration, and spiritual nourishment. Live erotically! Find kernels of passion in each passing moment and turn them into erotically charged interactions with your partner. Those erotic interactions will keep churning the potentially perpetual mechanism of your "Passionately Hereafter."

Sex Rx Rule: *Live erotically! Pursue passion in everyday life and then turn it into desire for your partner.*

PART I

THE PRIORITY FACTOR: DAYS 1–6

CHAPTER 1

Committing to the Program

You're probably tired of keeping your sex life on the back burner, but don't quite know what to do about it. Because of the demands of daily life, sex ends up on the bottom of your to-do list—somewhere after visiting the in-laws and cleaning out the garage. You may view romance and passion as a luxury rather than a necessity, akin to a tropical vacation you can only afford once in a while.

WHY SEX SUFFERS

You're not alone. Many couples experience a sexless, passion-less coexistence. Among the many causes are overworking, relational issues, and lack of time, energy, and privacy. Most couples are burdened with baggage: dual careers, financial pressures, demanding children, or elderly relatives needing care— too many responsibilities, not enough breaks. People spend their leisure time on their BlackBerrys, iPods, iPads, the Internet, e-mail, and social networking instead of in bed.

Yet research shows that sex is much more than a mere act of procreation or pleasurable release. Sex improves your mood, burns calories, relieves pain, boosts your immunity, prolongs your life, reduces stress, and improves your relationship. Sex is crucial to your relationship as it releases the hormone oxytocin, which makes you feel closer and more connected, deepening your love bond. And you don't need any studies to tell you that sex is fun!

One study found that for the average American, increasing the frequency of intercourse from once a month to once a week generates happiness equivalent to getting an additional $50,000 in income! The economists who conducted that study also estimated that a lasting marriage equated to the happiness generated by an extra $100,000 per year. It is clear that taking steps to improve your sex life is worth your time and effort.

MISGUIDED BELIEFS ABOUT SEX

Many couples hold the belief that sex should be spontaneous to be good. In fact, research shows that for couples in long-term relationships, planning a romantic interlude leads to a higher-quality, more enjoyable sexual experience. Of course, this doesn't mean a couple should pass up an opportunity for a "quickie" if one presents itself. It means proactively setting the stage and creating circumstances conducive to passionate lovemaking.

Each couple needs to evaluate their environment and determine the optimal conditions for great sex. For example, many parents have trouble turning off their parenting brains when their children are around—even if the kids are fast asleep. Similarly, many workaholics have trouble switching off their cognitive brains and being fully mindful of their partner.

In order to restore the erotic connection, you might need to find a way to put some distance between yourself and your kids or to leave your Blackberry in your car—that can do wonders for your sex life. Planning a romantic evening allows time to eliminate all of the variables that interfere with your maximum enjoyment of each other and to create what we call "conditions for optimal arousal."

CHEMISTRY IS NEVER ENOUGH

Another fallacious belief many couples hold is that sexual chemistry is all you need to have passion for each other. Chemistry is that initial intense and inexplicable sexual attraction you feel when you first meet your partner. Chemistry also has a truly chemical component; some research suggests that pheromones, invisible and odorless airborne molecules that the body gives off to attract sexual partners, influence our selection of who turns us on. Chemical attraction is impossible to fake or create, and it often persists even if the couple is otherwise incompatible.

Although sexual chemistry is what brings most couples together initially, it is only part of the formula for passion in a long-term relationship. You can be intensely attracted to your partner, yet fail to get along or fulfill each other's emotional or sexual needs. And even though sexual chemistry is crucial in the beginning of the relationship, its intensity fades when you spend time together. So, in addition to chemistry, you need to be committed and compatible, as well as willing to communicate and compromise, in order to have a satisfying sex life.

MAKING THE COMMITMENT

Bringing back the passion of prior days requires commitment. There's a difference between staying in a relationship because you don't want to deal with the consequences of getting out (constraint commitment) and being together because you feel gratification from investing in the relationship (dedicated commitment). Expressing dedicated commitment to each other builds trust, motivation, and a desire to reconnect. You express commitment when you fulfill your promises, when you make mutual plans for the future and set common goals for the relationship, when you remember things that are important for your partner, and when you commemorate the anniversary of your marriage or meeting.

If you feel you or your partner has a fear of commitment that prevents you from fully dedicating yourself to the current relationship, consider addressing this issue in individual therapy. Whether your commitment phobia stems from fear of being engulfed or fear of being abandoned, you will not be able to benefit fully from this program, or have a truly satisfying sex life, without the trust, safety, and security achieved through dedicated commitment.

IMPROVING YOUR COMMUNICATION

Clear and fair communication is essential to healthy relationships. Relationship satisfaction depends on having your needs met, and your partner cannot fulfill your needs if you are not clear about expressing them. Let your partner know what you need from the relationship by making specific requests, such as "I really need you to help me change the baby's diapers, as I feel overwhelmed having to do it myself all the time."

Communication also requires mutual disclosure. Listen to your partner when he or she needs to confide in you, and confide in your partner. When you listen to your partner speak, engage in active listening. Acknowledge the content of what your partner says and reflect your partner's feelings with statements such as, "You feel very frustrated about working with such insensitive people."

Clear communication also involves discussing disagreements as they inevitably arise instead of repressing or glossing over them. It's a fallacy that happy couples do not fight—all couples occasionally do—but functional couples "fight fair." When you express your complaint, focus on your partner's specific behavior and how it makes you feel, such as "I feel angry when you are late for dinner and don't call to let me know." Listen to your partner's response without interrupting.

When you do respond, stay focused on the topic. Do not bring up past complaints, hurts, and the kitchen sink. If you feel the argument is escalating out of your control, terminate it by saying "Stop action!" and take a break from each other's physical presence. Clear communication is something that requires continued practice before it becomes habitual.

WORKING ON BEING COMPATIBLE

In addition to chemistry, commitment, and clear communication, you need to be compatible to maintain passion. Compatibility requires some degree of commonality in your core beliefs, such as religion, family structure, and philosophy of life. It is hard to sustain passion when your life goals are clearly incompatible—one partner wants to have a big family, another partner wants to remain childless. Compatibility may also include some complementary differences—one partner can't boil an egg, the other loves to cook—the kinds of differences that enhance the relationship.

Sexual compatibility involves having a similar degree of sexual desire and preference. The issue of sexual compatibility often comes up when a couple suffers from the desire discrepancy—having dramatically different levels of sexual desire or preferring different sexual activities. The more-sexual partner often feels ignored and shortchanged, while the less-sexual one often feels harassed and bullied into having sex. It is easy to see each perspective if you think of sex as akin to other physiological needs, such as hunger—one person is starving and the other is being force-fed. Couples with desire discrepancies need to clarify their needs, compromise, and cooperate.

PRACTICING COMPROMISE AND COOPERATION

No relationship can survive without constant compromise and cooperation. No matter how compatible you are with your partner, sometimes your desires or goals will not be congruent. Dismissing one partner's needs for the sake of the other's always leads to resentment and the eventual breakdown of the relationship.

How do you practice compromise and cooperation? Take, for example, the common problem of desire discrepancy, described earlier. To compromise and cooperate in solving this problem, your first step is to determine how often each of you would like to have sex and the types of sexual activities you would prefer. See if you can find a middle ground. Try to figure out the best way to meet the needs of both parties.

For example, maybe you can trade having sex more often for having a wider variety of sexual activities less often. You may need to subordinate some of your needs for the sake of the relationship, such as succumbing to the sexual advances of your partner when you are not in the mood or choosing self-pleasuring instead of intercourse while your partner watches. The question to consider is: What is best for me versus what is best for our relationship, and how can a compromise be reached?

The Erotic Memory Lane
Use these questions to remember why you and your partner fell in love with each other:

1. What was your first thought when you saw your partner?
2. When did you have your first erotic thought about your partner?
3. When did you first kiss and who initiated it?
4. When was the first time you made love and what was it like?

5. What do you remember most about your first months together?
6. What did you find most appealing sexually about your partner?
7. What did you find most appealing physically about your partner?
8. What did you find most appealing emotionally about your partner?
9. What was your favorite vacation with your partner?

Sex Rx Rule: *Empower your passion by giving it priority.*

Insight for Him and Her: Make Your Relationship a Priority

Your relationship has to become your priority. Nothing should trump your dedication to each other: Children, parents, friends, jobs, talents, and even health are all secondary to the emphasis you should put on your relationship. That means getting a present for your wife before getting one for your daughter, and returning your husband's phone call before that of your mother. It means taking a lower-paying but flexible job that allows you to spend more time with your spouse and not turning down your partner's request for intimacy even if you do have a headache. It means learning to say no to nonessential demands on your time.

DAY 1

On the first day of your program, focus on making a commitment to improving your sex life and bringing back passion and romance. Research shows that out of 100 well-intentioned people who vow to stop smoking, lose weight, or save money, only twelve will succeed. How can you do better? By practicing the suggestions outlined below:

1. **Remind yourself why sex is important to you.** Write a list and paste it in your planner or print it out and attach it to your computer screen. Your list may go something like this:

   If I have better sex:
   - I will be less cranky and feel happier.
   - I will make my partner happier and healthier.
   - I will be thinner and more flexible.
   - I will be less likely to catch a cold.
   - I will be less likely to have cancer.
   - I will have more regular periods/a better prostate.
   - I will live a longer, healthier life.
   - I will feel closer to my partner.
   - I will have a happier marriage.

2. **Once you've made a commitment to yourself, discuss it with your partner.** Make sure you both agree about the importance of improving your sex life and are willing to carve out time for the program. If your schedules are really hectic, pull out a calendar and schedule a date night two weeks from today. If your partner feels awkward having to schedule sex, think of it as a quality time night and discuss what you would like to do together—go to a restaurant of his or her choosing, see a show, get a couples massage, or rent a movie and stay in—so long as you can eliminate distractions such as work, children, and pets for that evening. As you will see, some of the exercises in this book will be set in the context of a date night. Having this

quality time with each other is crucial. Research shows that it is not the toughest of life's trials, such as illness or job loss, that break up relationships, but trivial busyness and mundane boredom that make couples grow apart.

3. **Look over and sign the Contract of Enhancement of Erotic Union.** It is not a legal document, but a type of behavioral contract used by psychologists to increase patient motivation.

CONTRACT OF ENHANCEMENT OF EROTIC UNION

THIS AGREEMENT is entered into this _____ day of_____ , 20 _____ by and between _____ hereinafter referred to as "Partner 1," and _____ hereinafter referred to as "Partner 2."

WHEREAS both parties recognize that true love means caring for the other and for the other's well-being and happiness;

WHEREAS both parties acknowledge and agree that sexual satisfaction is essential to a person's well-being and happiness; and

WHEREAS both Partner 1 and Partner 2 acknowledge their love for each other and desire to enhance their love and their union by maximizing their mutual sexual satisfaction and enjoyment;

NOW, THEREFORE, Partner 1 and Partner 2 hereby agree as follows:

In furtherance of the aforementioned, both parties agree to undertake and complete the 30-Day Sex Rx Program outlined in this book, which includes daily exercises to be performed alone and together. In that regard, both Partner 1 and Partner 2 agree that

(a) they will make their best effort to fulfill each of the assigned exercises in a timely and enthusiastic manner;

(b) they will not quit if they get behind in their assignments, but will persevere to complete them as expeditiously as possible in the time they have available;

(c) they will not draw premature conclusions about the efficacy or value of any exercise or portion of the Sex Rx Program until they have fully completed the program; and

(d) they will, in performing their exercises, maintain a loving and caring mindset toward the other party to this Contract.

The parties hereto, represent to each other that they are of sound mind and body and enter into this contract voluntarily with no undue coercion or duress; and said representations shall survive the making and entering into of this Contract.

Signed
Partner 1 _____
Partner 2 _____

Although this is not a legally binding contract, putting your intentions down on paper and signing them motivates you to stick to your resolutions. People like to keep their promises, especially when they're clearly stated. No, you won't be able to sue your partner if he forgets to leave you a naughty message or reneges on your date night, but he will probably feel bad for breaching your contract and will work extra hard to make it up to you. The contract also affirms your dedication to improving your sex life.

4. **Conclude your contract signing with a handshake.**
Begin with a firm handshake, but then soften it and make
this handshake linger for a while, feeling the warmth of
your partner's hand while gazing into his eyes. Gently
squeeze your partner's hand and try to recall what it felt
like to hold her hand for the first time. Feel the heat
of your partner's hand and visualize the energy passing
between you. You have just made a pact to become the
best lovers you can be—sexual soulmates.

5. **Hug each other for thirty seconds (*huggus uninterruptus,* as we call it).** Hugging has tremendous health
benefits. A twenty-second hug lowers stress hormones,
including cortisol, and increases oxytocin, a "warm and
fuzzy" hormone associated with familial love, which lowers blood pressure and reduces stress. Oxytocin sensitizes
skin to touch, encourages affection, and deepens the
bond of love. It also has an amnesic effect on us as it
blocks negative memories. It is released during childbirth
and breastfeeding to make a new mother forget the pain
and sleepless nights, and focus on her bond with the infant.
That's why frequent touching is important in keeping passion alive. Resist the urge to break the hug—instead, stay
in the hug long enough to deeply relax your body and
your mind. Remember, no sexual touching tonight!

DAY 1 SUMMARY

- Create a list of reasons why improving your sex life is
  paramount to you.
- Get your partner interested in and committed to the pro-
  gram, and schedule your first date two weeks from today.
- Sign the Contract of Enhancement of Erotic Union.
- Practice thirty seconds of *huggus uninterrruptus.*

DAY 2

On the second day, continue to solidify your commitment to the program by reconnecting with your initial lust for each other, writing it down, and sharing it with each other. You'll also share with your friends and relatives your intention to bring back the passion in your relationship, thus laying the groundwork for reducing distractions.

1. **Schedule an annual health checkup for you and your partner, and ask your doctor to check your hormone levels.** If you feel that your level of sexual desire has declined over the years, make sure to bring it up with your gynecologist or urologist. Blood pressure, diabetes, thyroid problems, and other conditions can all contribute to libido blues. This is also the time to check your meds. Many prescription medications can be libido killers, including antidepressant, diabetes, allergy, ulcer, birth control, and blood pressure drugs. Some can also contribute to erectile dysfunction in men.

2. **Pull out old photo albums, cards, and scrapbooks and review them, then start jotting down notes about qualities that initially attracted you to each other.** Think of all the reasons you fell in love with your partner and list as many of them as you can. Call this the List of Reasons.

   - The first thing I noticed about you was . . .
   - The first thing that attracted me to you was . . .
   - You made me smile when you . . .
   - I knew I loved you when . . .

3. **To solidify your commitment, recall the intense passion of your first days together.** To help you

re-experience that passion so that you crave it again, complete a List of Turn-Ons.

- My heart skipped when I first saw your (smile, legs, naked body, smiled at me, et cetera)
- I felt those butterflies in my stomach when you (nibbled on my neck, et cetera)
- I got so turned on when you (touched my hand, French-kissed me, et cetera)
- I got goose bumps when you (whispered in my ear, caressed my neck, et cetera)

Be as explicit as you can. You want to start reconnecting with those feelings of lust and passion that initially attracted you to each other. Your desire to get back what you once felt in each other's presence will keep you motivated to stick with the program.

4. **Tell everyone about your commitment to improving your sex life with your partner.** Call it The Better Sex Solution Project. E-mail your friends and relatives about it. Tell them you will be busy for the next thirty days improving your sex life and will not be checking your e-mail as often as usual. Post your resolution to bring back your passion on Facebook and Twitter. Research shows that sharing your commitment to change with others makes it more likely that you will stick with it.

5. **Hold each other as you drift off to sleep while abstaining from direct sexual contact.** Turn to each other, aligning your chests. Gaze into each other's eyes for a few minutes, mentally recalling the first time you met. Before you fall asleep, share with each other the List of Reasons and List of Turn-Ons you compiled. You don't have to memorize the lists verbatim, just

recall a few of the most important items from each list. Then turn around and fall asleep in the spooning position. Remember, no sexual touching tonight!

DAY 2 SUMMARY

- Schedule an appointment for you and your partner to see a physician and undergo hormonal testing.
- Write down a list of qualities that attracted you to each other, as well as a list of things that your partner did to turn you on during the most passionate stage of your relationship.
- Solidify your commitment to the program by sharing with others your intent to improve your sex life with your partner.
- Recite these lists to each other while snuggling before drifting off to sleep.

CHAPTER 2

Releasing Your Libido

Now that you're fully committed to improving your sex life, you need to start focusing on boosting your libido. First and foremost you must have desire before you can be motivated to have sex, to feel aroused, to orgasm, and to feel overall sexual satisfaction. Libido is dependent on the overall health and functioning of your body.

When you are sleep-deprived, tired, lethargic, ill, or lacking energy, you're not likely to want sex. That's why your lifestyle is critical in maintaining a strong sexual desire. Healthy sleeping and eating habits and moderate exercise unleash your sexual lust, whereas greasy, processed foods, lack of sleep, and a sedentary lifestyle erode your libido. Lazy folks have lousy sex!

BETTER DIET, BETTER LIBIDO

Most of us have heard the expression "You are what you eat." This adage rings true when it comes to your sex life, too. Your diet has a deep impact on your sexual health. An unhealthy, fast-food diet not only puts on unwanted pounds (which make you feel unsexy and undesirable), it clogs your arteries (reducing blood flow to your genitals) and makes you feel apathetic, lethargic, and too tired to have sex.

Weight loss is correlated with a significant increase in libido, particularly in women.

Practice these health steps to keep your libido high:

- Because energy is important for good sex, prior to jumping in the sack, eat high-protein foods such as fish, chicken, low-fat dairy products, or beans.
- Reduce processed foods, sugars, and simple carbohydrates. You'll feel light and have more energy, and you may even shed those unwanted pounds. In addition, many processed foods contain substances called phytoestrogens, which lower testosterone, a hormone responsible for sexual desire in men and women.
- Eat fish rich in omega-3 fatty acids, such as salmon (or take fish oil capsules), which lowers LDL and elevates dopamine, the libido-boosting chemical.
- Boost testosterone (a libido-enhancing hormone) by eating peanut butter as well as oysters and other foods that are high in zinc. Eating brown rice and red meat curbs the production of prolactin, which reduces testosterone. Honey contains the mineral boron, which enhances testosterone levels.
- Long considered the original aphrodisiac, chocolate not only has an appealing taste, it contains phenythylamine, or PEA, the "love chemical." It also contains theobromine, a substance similar to caffeine. Too much chocolate will cause a spike in blood sugar and make you sleepy, so a little goes a long way. Dark chocolate has more PEA and less milk and sugar than milk chocolate, so choose that. Cheese also contains PEA, as do apples and almonds.
- Drink a cup of coffee. In moderation (and when it doesn't interfere with your ability to get a good night's sleep), caffeine increases dopamine, a brain neurotransmitter that plays a role in feeling pleasure, including sexual pleasure. But don't overdo your java—too much

caffeine will act as a vasoconstrictor, restricting blood flow to your genitals and other parts of your body.

- Foods that improve circulation can help you increase genital arousal. These foods include olives, olive oil, garlic, nuts, ginger root, and beans.

- If you like spicy food, use chili peppers to heat up your sex life. They contain capsaicin, which stimulates nerve endings to release chemicals that raise the heart rate and trigger the release of endorphins.

- Nutmeg has been empirically proven to stimulate libido in male rats by increasing their erections and mounting frequency after the rats consumed it for seven days. Why not give it a try and see if it does the same for you? Although there is no specific recommended dose for a human male, you can add some nutmeg to your morning cereal or sprinkle some on your salad to add a little spice to your sex life.

FOODS AND CHEMICALS TO AVOID

Aspartame (found in many diet foods and diet soft drinks), nicotine, and alcohol are vasoconstrictors, meaning they restrict blood flow, including blood flow to the genitals, which may make it difficult for a man to achieve and sustain a satisfying erection. Avoid vasoconstrictors for at least six to twelve hours before sex. Other common substances that may diminish sexual performance in men include cold, allergy, or sinus medicines; aspirin; antihistamine; lemon juice; and vinegar. Both men and women should avoid carbohydrates and L-tryptophan-rich foods such as turkey, which will temporarily turn you into a couch potato.

GET MORE EXERCISE TO GET MORE SEX

Research has shown that women who exercise on a regular basis tend to have more active sex lives, are more easily aroused, and reach orgasms more quickly than those who do not exercise. For men, erectile dysfunction is highly correlated with poor physical health and inactivity. More than 50 percent of men with diabetes and 44 percent of those with high blood pressure had trouble achieving an erection, and so did the 26 percent of subjects who reported such sedentary behavior as watching three or more hours of television per day.

Regular exercise not only helps increase blood flow to the genitals, it releases endorphins and lowers cortisol levels, both of which help reduce stress. Exercise delivers even more benefits when performed with your partner.

All types of physical exercise lead to enhanced sexual desire and performance, but exercises that improve stamina and flexibility in the pelvic area are particularly beneficial for improving your sex life. So in addition to regular workouts, you and your partner might want to engage in exercises specifically developed to enhance your sexual performance—we call them sexercises. We have included the most commonly practiced ones, but you can certainly modify them and make up your own.

DOUBLE DOWNWARD DOG

Get on all fours, with your knees under your hips and your hands flat on the floor directly under your shoulders. Your partner should stand behind you. Lift your knees off the floor, put your weight on the balls of your feet, and draw your behind backward so that your back, arms, and head form a straight line. Slowly straighten your legs so that your hips rise up as you press your heels down on the floor. Keep your head down. You should look like an upside-down V. Your partner should place one leg between your legs for balance, then grab the sides of your hips from behind and pull them back for a deeper stretch. Hold this position for five to ten deep breaths, then switch positions with your partner.

DOUBLE FLYING BUTTERFLY

Sit on the floor with your knees bent and have your partner kneel directly behind you. Put the soles of your feet together in front of you and place your hands over your toes. Have your partner place his or her hands on the insides of your thighs, just above your knees. Keeping your back flat, slowly lean forward as far as you can as your partner gently pushes your legs down toward the floor. Hold this pose for five to ten deep breaths, then switch places with your partner.

DOUBLE ROWING BOAT

Sit on the floor directly across from your partner. Both of you should spread your legs as wide apart as possible, touching your feet to your partner's. Reach forward and grab each other's wrists or elbows so that your arms are straight and locked together. From this position, slowly lean back while your partner bends forward at the waist as far as is comfortable. Hold for two to three deep breaths. Both of you should keep your backs straight throughout the exercise. Next, let your partner lean back. This time, you'll bend at the waist toward him or her and hold for two to three deep breaths. Repeat this back-and-forth movement five to ten times.

KEGEL EXERCISES

Even more important than sexercises are exercises for your pelvic muscles, known as Kegel exercises, or "Kegeling." These were originally developed as a treatment for urinary incontinence in women but have been shown to improve sexual arousal and orgasm intensity in both women and men. These exercises stimulate the pubococcygeal (or PC) muscles, which stop the flow of urine midstream (not the muscles used to hold in your stomach or tighten your buttocks).

To practice Kegels, contract your PC muscle by clenching, as though stopping urine, and hold for at least two to three seconds per squeeze. Inhale as you squeeze each time and try to fully relax your muscles between each contraction. Start with fifteen squeezes, twice daily, gradually increasing the number of Kegels until you can comfortably do sixty at a time. Then begin holding each contraction for a count of three.

After a month or so, these exercises will become automatic and almost effortless and you'll start noticing results. If you're a woman, you'll be able to grasp your partner's penis with your vaginal muscles, intensifying pleasure for both of you; if you're a man, you can delay ejaculation by contracting your PC muscle just before orgasm, and then fully relaxing them. Many women report enhanced orgasms using this technique, and some men report being able to achieve multiple orgasms.

For Women

An easy way to locate the vaginal muscles is to sit on the toilet and start to urinate, then start and stop the flow of urine midstream. You're using your PC muscle to do that. Another way to identify the correct muscle group is to insert a finger into your vagina and then try to tighten the muscles around your finger, keeping your abdominal and thigh muscles relaxed.

Once you've located the correct muscles, you can simply tighten and relax them over and over, optimally about 100 contractions once or twice a day. However, don't try to maximize this exercise at the outset. Work up to it in stages until you can do 100 easily without any strain—and make sure you do these on an empty bladder.

Although the easiest way to do Kegels is the rapid squeeze-release, there are several variations of this exercise. For superior results, try performing deliberately slow and focused contractions, called "elevator Kegels." Imagine that the ground floor is at the entrance to your vagina and the tenth floor is around your belly button. Slowly raise the elevator one floor at a time as you contract the PC muscle. You can hold the muscle tightened for five seconds, or you can imagine that you are drawing water up, like a siphon, into your vagina or trying to eject something from your vagina by bulging the muscles out at the end.

Try performing these exercises in various positions: lying on your back with your knees bent (you can put a pillow under your buttocks so that your vagina lifts up a little); on all fours (raise while squeezing and then lower yourself when relaxing); and squatting (you can raise and lower your lower abdomen and squeeze when moving up). Make sure not to hold your breath as this can cause a headache; instead, try to breathe out as you squeeze the muscles.

Some women find it easier to use a vibrator or a dildo to create resistance and do the contractions against them. The newer, anatomically realistic–looking dildos made of silicone and jelly-like substances are good for Kegels, as they offer springy resistance. A disposable douche can also be effectively used for Kegels. While standing in the shower (or over the toilet), insert the nozzle of the douche and then try to hold the container with your vaginal muscles. You can fill the bottles with different amounts of water and slowly work your muscles up to holding a full bottle. You can also purchase Kegel instruments online.

For the best results, you need to exercise on a regular basis. If you already have a daily exercise program for your body, you can add the Kegel exercises to that program. Most women will notice changes after just three weeks of regular Kegeling. The easiest way to measure change is to insert your finger and contract your vaginal muscles around it—or practice contracting during intercourse and ask your partner whether your squeezes on his penis are getting stronger.

Kegeling improves intercourse not only for the partner of the women who practice these techniques but also for the women themselves. Women who practice daily Kegels report increased length and strength of their vaginal orgasms, and some even report that Kegeling provides indirect stimulation of their clitoris.

For Men

PC muscle exercises can help men gain greater control over their erections and delay ejaculation. Most men who have strengthened these muscles report stronger erections, more powerful ejaculations, more explosive orgasms, and healthier prostates. Many men who complain that their ejaculate just dribbles out are able to increase the power of their ejaculation through PC muscle exercises. Women also have reported enjoying the feeling of a man flexing his penis inside the vagina when he contracts the PC muscle.

One end of the male PC muscle can be felt behind the testicles, around the base of the scrotum. Men can learn to contract this muscle in the same way women learn—by practicing cutting off the flow of urine. This exercise can be done whether or not you are experiencing an erection at the time, by squeezing the muscle up to ten times in rapid succession. The other end of the PC muscle is located around the anus and can be felt when squeezing your muscles as if trying to prevent yourself from passing gas. Practice the posterior squeezes rapidly five to ten times in a row, being conscious of relaxing your anus after every squeeze. Try not to squeeze your thighs, butt, or ab muscles.

Training PC muscle allows a man to stop the flow of seminal fluid into the penis, thus delaying ejaculation and prolonging intercourse. Some men are able to achieve incredible control over their PC muscle, such as being able to withdraw the penis entirely in the pelvic cavity. The techniques focused on achieving male multiple orgasms are also premised on PC muscle control, such as being able to stop ejaculation and have a dry orgasm. The Tantric sex and Karezza techniques discussed in the last part of this book also require PC muscle control.

SENSATE FOCUS

Practicing sensate focus will help you to unleash your libido. This is a particular kind of undemanding sensual touch developed by sex researchers Masters and Johnson. The goal is to focus on the sensations of touch, nothing more.

A sensate-focus touch is very slow, free of pressure to perform or respond, and is done for your pleasure. It is best performed with eyes closed and without talking. You should take turns touching each other. When you're the active partner (the one doing the touching), gently caress your partner and keep your attention on the areas where your skin touches your partner's. When you're the passive partner (accepting the touching), relax and mentally follow your partner's hand as it touches your body. Sensate focus will slowly but surely reawaken your libido.

Before starting sensate focus, remove any rings; if your hands are cold, hold them under a stream of warm water or rub them together vigorously.

DAY 3

On the third day, focus on modifying your lifestyle to release your hidden libidinal prowess. Increase your general physical activity level and choose an activity to perform with your partner for at least fifteen minutes daily, such as walking, swimming, or dancing together. Today you should also review your dietary and snacking habits and try to include a few aphrodisiacs in your diet, including herbs and vitamins.

1. **Increase your physical activity level.** Aim for at least thirty minutes of exercise three times per week and try to combine aerobic exercise (which strengthens the cardiovascular system) with muscle training (which builds strength and releases testosterone). Choose at least one physical activity that you can do with your partner. Exercising together has been shown to improve relationships, in part because doing so allows you to communicate in a side-by-side (as opposed to face-to-face) interaction, which men tend to find less confrontational. Here are some ideas for couples exercises:

   - Walking/hiking
   - Jogging/running
   - Dog walking
   - Geocaching
   - Swimming/water aerobics
   - Stretching
   - Yoga/tai chi
   - Spinning/cycling
   - Pilates/Swedish ball
   - Kickboxing/karate
   - Weight training
   - Skiing/skating
   - Horseback riding
   - Rock climbing
   - Aerobics/Zumba
   - Rafting/boating/kayaking
   - Snorkeling/scuba diving
   - Basketball/volleyball/soccer
   - Ballroom dancing/belly dancing/striptease
   - Exercise videos/Wii Fit

2. **Keep a brief food diary to track what you consume.**
   You may be surprised to see how many unhealthy food
   choices you make throughout the day. Sometimes
   making a few changes, such as detouring around Star-
   bucks, can make a huge difference. Also, don't forget
   to take your vitamins and herbs, particularly if your
   diet doesn't reflect the recommended food pyramid.
   Your body needs natural nutrients for optimal sexual
   performance. Consider adding to your diet:

   - Omega-3s, in conjunction with an Ester-C supple-
     ment, zinc, and vitamin D, can aid circulation and
     overall wellness—which equals better sex!
   - Vitamin E increases oxygen in your system, which
     improves overall blood flow, and is considered by
     many to be an aphrodisiac.
   - Iodine, SOD, selenium, RNA/DNA, manganese,
     bromelain, L-cysteine, choline, and inositol also
     play a role in healthy sexual desire by affecting hor-
     mones or blood flow, so make sure your multivita-
     min supplement contains these substances.
   - Many herbs have been found to enhance libido,
     including yohimbe bark, arugula, tribulus, dami-
     ana, ginseng, gingko biloba, kelp, balut, borojo,
     maca, and, of course, horny goat weed! Some of
     these boost levels of testosterone, the lust hormone;
     others increase dopamine, the motivation/mood
     enhancer hormone; and others enhance blood
     flow to the pelvic area. Consult a nutritionist or
     an herbal specialist before supplementing your diet
     with these herbs as they can be dangerous if not
     taken appropriately.

3. **Perform ten minutes of sensate-focus exercises (five minutes for each partner).** Focus on your partner's head and neck (this releases endorphins and relieves stress). Find an uninterrupted time and a quiet place, preferably your bedroom, and get into comfortable non-seductive clothes.

   One of you should sit with your head against the wall or back of the bed or couch. The other should lie down on your partner's lap and let your partner massage your head. You can play with your partner's hair, or try kneading, sweeping strokes, or light scratching on the scalp. From the head, move your touch to your partner's neck. Remember to touch very slowly and focus on the sensation of touch, not on trying to please your partner. After sensate focus, hold each other and drift off to sleep. No sexual touching tonight!

DAY 3 SUMMARY

- Review the list of physical exercises listed above and decide which ones you will engage in alone and together.
- Track your daily nutrition, make healthy changes in your diet, and plan to add at least one aphrodisiac to your menu daily.
- Stop by a health food or vitamin store and choose some libido-enhancing herbs and vitamins.
- Perform ten minutes of sensate-focus exercises, concentrating on the head and neck.

Insight for Him: Low Testosterone = Low Libido
If your libido has been particularly lackluster lately, the cause may be a low testosterone level. You should suspect a low testosterone level if you have decreased

motivation not only for sexual activity but for other parts of your life as well; if you get fewer erections upon awakening; and if you have fewer spontaneous erections when you're feeling aroused. In those cases, consult your doctor. Your testosterone can be measured through a simple blood or saliva test and can be regulated with a gel, injection, or patch.

Insight for Her: Hormones and Low Libido

Decreased libido in women can also be caused by low testosterone levels. Some birth control pills may lower sexual desire by manipulating levels of testosterone and estrogen. Talk to your doctor—sometimes changing your birth control method can respark your libido. A postmenopausal drop in libido can also be caused by hormonal changes. Between the ages of forty-two and fifty-two, 50 percent of women lose interest in sex altogether, primarily because by age fifty women lose up to 70 percent of their testosterone. Many women benefit from hormone replacement therapy, which may include testosterone and/or estrogen supplementation, to renew their interest in sex. However, HRT is not for everyone as it carries a risk of pulmonary embolism, particularly in smokers, and may be associated with a slightly higher incidence of breast cancer, asthma, gallstones, migraine headaches, and seizures.

Bonus Points for Him: Helping with Household Chores

Who knew that doing the dishes could improve your sex life? Men have a tendency to overestimate how much they do around the house and underestimate how much other family members accomplish. Correcting that lack of balance helps remove the mental blocks that keep her from thinking about sex: the dirty kitchen, the soiled bathroom, the messy family room, the cluttered basement. A woman's house is her fortress—if it's untidy or disorderly, she feels vulnerable and defenseless. You can get a woman into the bedroom by performing above her expectations in every other room in the house.

DAY 4

Today, practice your sexercises and Kegeling. The sexercises are designed to awaken your passion and may be discontinued after you finish the program; however, you should continue Kegeling for a lifetime, as it is a wonderful tool for enhancing desire, sensations of arousal, and orgasm.

Continue to enhance your libido by eliminating desire-downers such as recreational drugs, nicotine, and excessive alcohol. Finally, adjust your schedule so that you get enough sleep—when you're sleep-deprived, sleep seems preferable to sex!

1. **Continue practicing sexercises and begin Kegeling.** Try to do Kegel exercises three or four times a day, varying the intensity of your squeezing and the amount of time you hold the squeeze in a set. In a few days, you'll notice that Kegels change the way your sexual excitement and your orgasms feel.

2. **Drop the oral obsession**—and by that we don't mean oral sex, of course! Quit smoking. Period. Although it was once de rigueur to sport a cigarette or cigar in your

hand, it's no longer in vogue. It poisons not only you but also your loved ones, your pets, and the environment—smoking is bad, bad, bad, for you and your sex life. It's a vasoconstrictor, which means it reduces blood flow to your genitals, lessening the rigidity of male erections and female engorgement. In one study of impotent men, more than a third resolved their problem simply by giving up cigarettes for six weeks.

3. **Limit your alcohol consumption.** Although small amounts of alcohol have a positive impact on sexual desire and arousal, if men drink too much, they may have difficulty getting erections, and both men and women may have difficulty experiencing orgasm. Research shows that even a few drinks may reduce your sexual response. If you find that alcohol relaxes you and reduces your inhibitions, stick with a glass or two of alcohol per day, sipped slowly with your partner, savoring every drop. Red wine has been shown to be an aphrodisiac because it is high in antioxidants, so if you like to sip wine with your partner, go red.

4. **Say no to illicit drugs.** Street drugs may initially enhance desire and loosen inhibitions, but in the long run they inhibit performance and reduce orgasmic feelings. Cocaine damages pleasure receptors in the brain. Marijuana and opiates deaden nerve endings, decreasing your ability to get turned on and to feel orgasm. If getting high is something you do as a couple, make a commitment to quitting or greatly reducing the amount of recreational drugs you consume. Take your pick—get stoned or get turned on!

5. **Catch up on your ZZZs.** Sleep deprivation leads to lower libido as well as weight gain, irritability, and difficulty focusing. Most sleep-deprived people choose slumber over a sex romp. Individual sleep needs may

vary, but aim to get the recommended six to eight hours per night. If you find yourself falling asleep the moment you get into bed with your partner, you need to catch up on your slumber. Cut down on the java, skip the late show, hit the snooze button, and get your much-needed rest so that you and your partner can have the energy for exercise and lovemaking. If you suffer from insomnia, consult your physician—or at least the local health food store, where you can pick up natural sleep remedies such as melatonin spray.

6. **Perform ten minutes of sensate-focus exercises (five minutes each).** Today, focus on the shoulders, upper back, and arms. Your arms contain specific nerve endings known as C-tactile fibers. Stroking them activates areas of the brain involved in processing love, trust, and affection.

    Remember to touch slowly, for the sole purpose of touching. Don't put any pressure on yourself and don't seek your partner's feedback. There is no right or wrong way to touch during these exercises—you can use very light, grazing touching, or deeper, massage-like kneading strokes. After the exercises, hold each other tightly and drift off to sleep. Remember, no sexual contact tonight!

Bonus Points for Her: Wear High Heels

A recent study showed that wearing a pair of moderately high-heeled shoes had beneficial effects on a woman's sex life. Researcher Dr. Maria Cerruto reported that wearing heels works the pelvic muscles and thus reduces the need to exercise them. Another reason to wear high heels? They make you fitter and sexier. You burn twice as many calories walking in heels as in flats, and they make your legs appear longer. Research involving more than 200 men and women found that people whose legs are 5 percent longer than average are considered the most attractive, regardless of gender. And every woman instinctively knows from the Cinderella story that shoes have the power to transform her from a dull and overworked pauper into a glamorous and carefree princess.

Bonus Points for Him: Take Her Shoe Shopping

Women have long known the benefits of retail therapy—shopping releases dopamine, a mood-enhancing neurotransmitter that plays a role in sexual motivation. Apparently, for women shoe shopping is even more eroticized. In his book, *Sex on the Brain*, Dr. Daniel Amen writes, "In the brain, the sensory area of the foot is right next door to the sensory area of the clitoris. Unknowingly, women often feel that buying shoes is like foreplay." Men, you know what to do with this information! Take her on a shoe-shopping spree on a date night, then have her model her new acquisitions for you in a private fashion show staged in your bedroom.

DAY 4 SUMMARY

- Do your sexercises and Kegeling.
- If you abuse drugs, alcohol, or nicotine, begin working on a plan to quit or reduce consumption.
- Make sure to get sufficient sleep, as sleep deprivation is a major libido downer.
- Perform ten minutes of sensate-focus exercises, with emphasis on the shoulders, arms, and upper back.

CHAPTER 3

Reducing Distractions

We live in the world full of digital distractions perfectly designed for tuning out real flesh-and-blood human interactions. All those gadgets—from cell phones to iPods—prevent us from taking quiet, focused time for romance. The average American spends between four and five hours watching TV each day. One survey reported that 37 percent of Americans take their laptops to bed with them, and 30 percent interrupt sex to answer their cell phones. Almost 50 percent of British men said they would give up sex for six months in exchange for a free fifty-inch plasma television. And an Italian study showed that simply putting a television in the bedroom cut in half the amount of sex a couple had.

If you want to save your sex life, boot the boob tube from your bedroom (and from your life) and turn off your cell phone. When couples complain they don't have time for the exercises we assign to them, our advice is always simple: Cut down on television-viewing time!

Even if you're way below average in how much time you spend staring at the television, you can save a few hours per week by turning off the glimmering screen. Use the extra time to do the Sex Rx Program.

ELIMINATING ELECTRONIC DISTRACTIONS

Spending time online is another romance-robbing culprit. Forty-eight percent of Americans say they feel they're missing something important when they're offline and 28 percent say they spend less time socializing face-to-face because of the amount of time spent online. More than 20 percent of Americans admitted to having less sex so they can spend more time online.

Checking e-mail is addictive, and it distracts you from being focused on and connected to your partner. If you want to revive your romance, you need to value the importance of intercourse over Internet, real-partner touch over the iPod Touch. Try not to respond to most of the unimportant messages in your inbox for a week. We guarantee you'll discover you haven't missed much at all as a result of ignoring those e-mails. If you can't combat your connectivity obsession, then at least use it to e-mail sexy messages or send provocative pictures of yourself to your partner.

Although you may feel that surfing the Internet or watching TV helps you relax and unwind after a busy day, remember, you can either have a great sex life—or watch others have one! If you can't drop the flickering-screen obsession, choose a music channel on your television with melodies you and your partner both enjoy. The right music triggers relaxation and can lower your heart rate, blood pressure, and anxiety level. Find better ways to de-stress and unwind, such as giving each other a massage or drawing a bath for your partner.

RELAX AND REINVIGORATE

To fully experience sexual pleasure, you must free yourself from mental to-do lists, distance yourself from petty worries, and surrender your being to physical sensation. Jump-start this process by using a few relaxation techniques instead of zoning out in front of the television or laptop. Try sensate focus—if you don't turn it into foreplay, it can be very relaxing for both partners.

BREATHE TO FEEL PEACEFUL

Deep breathing helps dispel tension. Also known as belly breathing, deep diaphragmatic breathing involves expansion of the abdomen rather than the chest. The easiest way to do this is when you're lying down. Make sure you're wearing comfortable, nonconstricting clothes.

1. To breathe diaphragmatically, breathe in long, slow intakes of air, allowing the body to absorb all of the inhaled oxygen, and take twice as long to exhale. Concentrate on making each breath deep enough that your belly expands.

2. Place one hand on your abdomen and one on your chest as you inhale through your nose, letting your abdomen and the hand on your abdomen rise first.

3. Then exhale through your nose, allowing your abdomen and the hand on the abdomen to lower as your stomach pulls in and toward your back.

4. If you think your chest is moving too much, place your other hand on your chest—this hand should move less than the hand on your abdomen.

5. Begin by counting to 1 as you exhale and slowly work yourself up to 5. You don't need to count as you inhale.

6. Continue this exercise for 15 to 20 minutes, trying to make each breath a little slower and a little deeper.

After you learn to breathe with your diaphragm while lying down, practice doing it while standing, then while sitting down. Deep diaphragmatic breathing is the most challenging when you're in the sitting position, but you will get the hang of it with some practice.

FLEX YOURSELF RELAXED

If you feel a lot of muscular tension, perhaps from sitting at a desk all day, you may benefit from progressive muscle relaxation. Tense and relax each muscle in your body, starting with your toes and ending with your face.

1. Pick a time and place where you will not be disturbed and lie or sit in a comfortable position.
2. Close your eyes and tune in to your body, noticing which muscles are most tense.
3. Tighten, hold, and then relax one muscle group at a time. Begin with your toes: Tighten, hold, relax, breathe. Complete a breathing cycle—inhale and exhale once—before moving to the next muscle group.
4. Now do your ankles, then calves, thighs, up to your arms and wrists, then your jaw.
5. Finish by scrunching up your face: Hold, relax, breathe. One or two cycles should relax you.

TALK YOURSELF TRANQUIL

The relaxation technique known as autogenics involves "self-talk," a form of self-hypnosis that consists of encouraging each of your limbs to become warm, heavy, and relaxed.

1. Close your eyes and begin by telling yourself "I am at peace" or "I am relaxed and calm."
2. Then imagine increasing heaviness in your arms and legs as you mentally repeat, "My arms and legs are heavy" for 2 or 3 minutes. Conjure up any image that helps you create that feeling in your limbs, such as thinking that

your arm is as limp as a rag doll's or as heavy as lead. Feel the words rather than just saying them.

3. Mentally repeat, "My arms and legs are pleasantly warm" for 2 or 3 minutes.

4. Next, tell yourself, "My heartbeat is strong and calm," and feel your heartbeat become stronger and slower. Then repeat, "My breathing is slow and easy."

5. Continue the suggestions with the phrase "Pleasant warmth is radiating across my abdomen." Imagine a ball of sunshine at your solar plexus (about halfway between your belly button and your heart) radiating warmth and light across all your internal organs.

6. The final suggestion is "My face is cool" or "My forehead is cool." The coolness of your face should contrast with the warmth in your limbs and the core of your body, intensifying the depth of the autogenic state. At this point your body should be in a deeply relaxed state. This is when you can add any affirmations you like, such as "I feel my libido being released."

7. To end the autogenic session, flex your limbs, breathe deeply, and open your eyes.

COUNT YOURSELF CALM

To simplify the autogenics exercise, you can close your eyes and repeat a word or phrase that keeps your mind focused internally. You may repeat words such as "calm," "relax," "peace," or phrases that have a spiritual meaning to you. If you find it tedious to repeat the same word or phrase, count backwards instead. Start with a number, such as 50 or 100, depending on how much time you have, and count each breath as you exhale. You don't have to inhale immediately—you can rest comfortably before inhaling again. Don't worry if you lose track of the number, just continue counting from the last number you remember. This exercise is particularly helpful if your mind is spinning with endless concerns and to-do lists.

VISUALIZE YOURSELF SERENE

If you have difficulty tuning out the world around you, use visualization to conjure up a special place—a sanctuary or an oasis—where you are alone with your partner, perhaps floating on a cloud high above all earthly concerns. This relaxation technique is based on the principle that vividly imagining an experience triggers the same physiological responses that correspond with that experience in real life. Therefore, you should imagine a calm and relaxing experience.

1. Pick a time and place where you will not be disturbed.
2. Close your eyes and imagine yourself in your favorite place—it can be a real place you have visited, such as a spa, or an imaginary place, such as a secret garden.
3. Now use all of your senses to visually transport yourself there. You can mentally transmigrate into a mountain forest where you smell the pine trees, listen to the wind, walk with your lover, feel soft pine needles crunch under your feet, and then cuddle on a fuzzy blanket for a picnic. Or you can imagine being on the beach at sunset. Smell the ocean, hear the surf and the seagulls, taste the salty breeze, feel the grains of hot sand under your feet, see the golden rays of the setting sunlight illuminate your lover's face as you lean over for a kiss.

After you've practiced visualization for a while, your mind will respond by creating vivid and realistic scenes.

What the mind perceives, the mind believes! Switch off your dreary, stressful world and tune in to a self-created alternate reality.

WHEN CHILDREN DISTRACT YOU

Clearing distractions, distancing yourself from worries, and focusing on each other is particularly difficult if you have children—talk about distractions and libido dampeners! If you're the parent of a small child, you may feel guilty if you take time away from your child (or children) to be alone with your partner. This is especially true of mothers. You may be able to forget about your job when you get home (if you try), but parenting is a job that never ends.

However, remember that cultivating your connection with your partner is actually in the best interest of your children. That's because by paying attention to each other, you create the kind of cohesiveness that keeps families intact. Ideally, you should allocate a few hours each week to tête-à-tête time. Not everyone, of course, can abide by this rule at all times. The needs of a breast-feeding or cosleeping infant (not to mention a colicky one) may take temporary precedence over the needs of the couple.

But erotically charged couples find creative ways to maintain their passion even in less-than-ideal circumstances, such as when their bed turns into the location of a slumber party for their kids. If this happens to you, take your sexcapades to other parts of the house or sneak away to a hotel room. A lock on the door is probably the best way to ward off your little bedroom invaders.

Sex Rx Rule: Have a great sex life—or watch others pretend to have one on TV.

DAY 5

Set a relaxed mood in your household by eliminating electronic distractions and learning to de-stress and quiet your busy brain through breathing and relaxation techniques. Continue to engage in physical exercise and Kegeling, preferably while getting outdoors in the fresh air and sunshine. Finally, because you've been abstaining from intercourse for the last five days, start pleasuring yourself on a daily basis while fantasizing about your partner.

1. **Begin your bedroom makeover by eliminating digital distractions, such as laptops, day planners, and phones, particularly cell phones.** If you have a television in your bedroom, unplug it for now and cover it with a blanket or cloth to avoid the temptation to sneak a peek at your favorite show. You may use it later to watch erotica, but right now it's more important to learn to relax and focus on each other. Remove cell phone chargers from your bedroom so you won't be tempted to keep your phone close by.

   Clearing clutter from the bedroom is also important. Scattered clothes, overflowing drawers, and crumpled sheets are insidious libido-downers, particularly for women, whose multitasking minds have trouble tuning out the visual disorder in order to get turned on. So when the house needs tidying up, always begin with your bedroom, which should be your sensual oasis.

2. **Choose a stress-reduction strategy, such as deep diaphragmatic breathing, visualization, progressive muscle relaxation, or autogenics.** Or introduce white noise by playing a CD of nature sounds such as falling rain or crashing waves or by installing a water fountain in your bedroom.

3. **Get out of the house and take in some fresh air and sunshine.** If you're like most people, you associate your house with lots of responsibilities and to-do lists. Feeling cooped up and breathing recirculated air can cause drowsiness and fatigue, so air out your lungs—pumping your lungs full of oxygen will pump your desire.

   Going outside will not only get you away from the indoor temptation of digital distraction, it will let you reconnect with nature, the original aphrodisiac. When you're outside, feel the sun on your face. Although tanning has gotten a bad rap lately, moderate sun exposure puts you in the mood for sex by causing your body to release health-promoting vitamin D, as well as the pleasure endorphins and the sex-drive hormone testosterone. Sunlight also stimulates the release of serotonin and has been shown to increase libido. Is it any wonder that island folks are known to be hot and horny?

   Many of us feel down when we don't get enough sunshine, and some even suffer from seasonal affective disorder (SAD). Nothing kills desire faster than the blues.

   Make plans for getting fresh air on a regular basis, about fifteen to thirty minutes per day, preferably while exercising together. If the weather is good, plan a romantic outing together—a picnic or a hike in the woods. Maybe even sneak in some nude sunbathing on your balcony or in your backyard if you can—but don't forget your sunscreen because a painful sunburn can put a real "ouch" in your love life. Use sunscreen on your body only if you plan to spend more than fifteen minutes outside.

If you're unable to get outdoors, air out your bedroom frequently or install an ozone-generating machine to get that fresh-air feeling indoors. Using full-spectrum lighting has also been shown to be a mood and libido booster.

4. **Give yourself some self-love—masturbate!** Self-pleasuring is one of the most effective stress relievers and one of the best ways to improve your sex life. Research shows that couples report the most sexual enjoyment when they engage in self-pleasuring prior to or during intercourse. For now, you're taking a break from having sex with each other as you learn how to improve your libido and enhance your passion for each other. Instead, pleasure yourself by fantasizing about your partner while touching yourself.

   If including your partner in your fantasies interferes with your arousal, evoke your favorite fantasy and try to include your partner as either a participant or an observer in that fantasy. For instance, if your favorite fantasy features a hot stranger, include your partner as a voyeur who gets to watch your sizzling encounter with the stranger. For women, self-pleasuring is particularly important for enhancing libido, as 90 percent of women are able to orgasm through masturbation compared with only 30 percent of women climaxing during partnered sex. You can use your hands or a sex toy, such as a vibrator or Hitachi wand, which is easier for most women. You and your partner can even watch each other masturbate, but no mutual sexual touching tonight!

DAY 5 SUMMARY

- Begin your bedroom makeover by eliminating digital distractions, such as laptops and cell phones, and by unplugging your TV.
- Choose a stress-reduction strategy and practice it regularly.
- Continue to engage in physical exercise and Kegeling, and get fresh air and sunshine.
- Give yourself some self-pleasuring—alone for now, but fantasize about your partner.

Insight for Him: Give Her the Gift of Time

You may feel frustrated when it's hard to get her in a sexual mood after a long day. It takes longer for a woman to turn off her busy brain and get in the mood for lovemaking. Although male sexual desire is spontaneous, female sexual desire is receptive—it may lie dormant until the right conditions arise. For a woman to feel sexual, she has to feel sexy, which requires both physical preparation (rituals such as washing her hair or putting on her makeup) and emotional/mental preparation (her psychological state of mind). A man's sexual desire isn't affected by his lack of time to take a shower and shave, but a woman's is.

Thus, turning your partner into a sex goddess means giving her the gift of time to be able to turn off her busy brain and engage in whatever rituals make her feel sexy.

DAY 6

Continue to remove passion distractions from your surroundings. The more distractions you can eliminate, the more time you will have to engage in "sexploration": to do Kegeling or practice your sexercises, to give each other sensate-focus massages, and to explore your hidden sexual turn-ons.

1. **Make a list of tasks you do every day when you get home from work.** Rate them on a scale of importance from 1 to 10. Decide which ones can be eliminated or performed less frequently. Do you spend too much time on social networking sites? Do you talk on the phone too much? Can you cut down on the time you spend cleaning or organizing? If the task is essential, such as watching the children or walking the dog, can you hire help or delegate responsibility to another family member? Eliminate as many nonessential activities as you can and promise each other not to take on any more commitments for the next month.

2. **Continue your bedroom makeover by sensualizing your bedroom ambiance.** Does it offer total privacy—or can it benefit from an additional lock or heavier curtains? Is the lighting soft and warm? Is the bed comfortable for sex? Do you like the feel and look of the sheets? Go shopping for sexy bedroom items together, such as candles, pillows, or adult toys. Choose appealing scents (aromatherapy oils, air fresheners, scented candles) and keep them handy. Consider adding mirrors and a nice music system. If you don't have minors in the house, what about adding some tasteful erotic art or boudoir photography for your bedroom walls, or getting some sex furniture

or a stripper pole? Think of your bedroom as your sexual sanctuary, the gateway to passion. But remember, no sex right now!

3. **Practice mindfulness.** Mindfulness is simply paying close attention to what you're experiencing, a practice of moment-to-moment nonjudgmental awareness adopted from Buddhism. Mindfulness has been shown to reduce stress, calm the mind, and make us happier and more connected with others. Try to engage all your senses: Feel the textures, smell the air, take in the sights, and listen to the sounds around you. Consider learning how to meditate if you have trouble being mindful.

4. **Focus on eroticism.** It's easier to transition to a sensuous mood if you've thought about your lust for your partner throughout the day. Put your favorite photos of you and your partner around your workspace and carry them in your wallet. Take a sensuous photo of your partner with your mobile phone and peek at it during lunch. Touch yourself sensuously whenever you have a minute alone, fantasizing about your partner.

5. **Jot down how you like to be touched in a notebook called His and Her Pleasure Manual.** You will soon start sharing this with your partner. Change your passwords to suggestive and erotic terms such as "dome-69now" or "4nicate2night," and they will become constant reminders of the passion you hold for your partner. You can also develop a special love code and write stick-on notes for each other with coded messages of the naughty acts you're planning, such as "Tonight we will dig for the gold." Only you and your partner will know what it means!

6. **Perform ten minutes of sensate-focus massage exercises.** Today you should focus on your partner's legs and feet. Afterwards, spend a few more minutes massaging each other's feet a bit harder, looking for the reflexology points that correspond to various sexual body parts. There are numerous sites on the Internet dedicated to sexual reflexology that have detailed charts. Many couples discover that a good foot massage is a blissful experience—no wonder it was a topic of such ardent discussion in the movie *Pulp Fiction*. Afterwards, snuggle together and drift off to sleep, remembering the List of Reasons and the List of Turn-Ons and sharing them with each other.

DAY 6 SUMMARY

- Eliminate nonessential tasks, hire help, and delegate responsibility so that you'll have more time for each other.
- Make your bedroom more inviting by adding sensuous items such as silk sheets and scented candles.
- Learn to become mindful—fully present—when interacting with your partner.
- Keep eroticism on your mind by surrounding yourself with reminders of your passion.
- Perform ten minutes of sensate-focus exercises, concentrating on the legs and feet.

Insight for Him: Making Out Doesn't Have to Lead to Sex

You get the most enjoyment out of sex when you view it as a full-body experience rather than a genitally focused interaction. Many men view all physically intimate contact as a prelude to some form of sexual activity, a linear progression from physical intimacy to sexual foreplay to intercourse to orgasm. Instead, think of your woman's sexual desire as a furnace that you need to keep warm by consistent nonsexual contact. Then, when you're both ready for a sexual encounter, her passion is already halfway there because you've kindled it with hugs, kisses, and tender touches—and her passion will burn with greater intensity!

PART 2

THE INTIMACY FACTOR: DAYS 7–12

CHAPTER 4

Removing Emotional Barriers

Negative emotions keep intimacy and passion out of your life. Shame and guilt about your sexuality (possibly stemming from childhood or a negative prior relationship), as well as resentment, anger, or contempt toward your partner, need to be dealt with so that you can have real, liberating passion. Unresolved emotional conflicts put a damper on your desire.

Although this book is not intended to help you heal from major traumas or resolve deep conflicts, this chapter can offer you a glimpse into how your negative emotions impact your sexual satisfaction with your partner. Major emotional barriers to intimacy can only be resolved through individual or couples therapy, but many times less dramatic emotional barriers can be lifted through awareness and self-healing.

DEALING WITH NEGATIVE THINKING

You may feel ashamed of your imperfect body because you internalized childhood criticism or unrealistic societal standards of beauty. Any doubts you have about your desirability, attractiveness, or sexual performance will inhibit your sexual desire. If you dislike your body or yourself, you expect others to do the same. It becomes hard to feel sexually desirable or worthy of feeling sexual desire.

If you act inhibited, your partner may view you as less sexually desirable. Research shows that sexual confidence is the biggest turn-on for your partner, and it can only be achieved when you fully accept your body. The key to self-acceptance is learning to recognize negative self-evaluations and actively rebut them with positive affirmations. An affirmation is a short, positive statement you think, say aloud, and/or write. It should be worded in the present tense, as if the condition already exists, and should only include words that express the desired condition. Whenever you have a negative thought about your body (or your partner's), counter it with a positive affirmation. Your affirmations should be strong, positive, and nonjudgmental. For example, if you're obsessing about your extra roll of belly fat, tell yourself "Stop it!" and then follow with an affirmative statement that describes a quality you like about yourself, such as "My body is strong, healthy, and full of vitality and passion, and I like it."

If you've always had a negative view of your physicality, you may be dealing with a psychological issue such as body dysmorphia, a preoccupation with an imagined physical defect or a minor defect that others often cannot even see. Seeing a therapist could help you learn to accept your body as it is and love it for all the pleasure it can bring you.

GUILT IN SEXUAL RELATIONSHIPS

Feelings of shame affect how we feel about our own sexuality; guilt affects our sexual relationships with others. Guilt is based on fear of hurting, burdening, or disappointing another. A recent survey has shown that only about 60 percent of women report being sexually satisfied compared with about 80 percent of men. Too many women feel guilty if they admit to not being satisfied or ask for a different type of stimulation (they don't want to hurt their partner's feelings). Similarly, many men feel guilty or ashamed to ask their wife for sexual acts that they consider "dirty." Many men have trouble seeing their women as a sexual object once they become the mother of their children. As one client put it, "How can I ask my wife to blow me with the same mouth she uses to kiss our children good night?"

If you feel guilty or ashamed, you can't tell your partner how you would like to be pleasured, nor can you take your time to reach the ultimate arousal while your partner is pleasuring you or assertively ask that your sexual needs be met. Improving your sexual communication skills by openly sharing your sexual desires will help you get rid of sexual shame and guilt. For an excellent self-help book on dealing with shame and guilt, read *Sex Without Guilt in the Twenty-First Century*, by Dr. Albert Ellis, one of the most influential sexologists of all time.

THE DANGERS OF ANGER AND RESENTMENT

Anger and resentment can destroy passion even faster than guilt and shame. Collecting grievances against your partner kills passion—each gripe is like a dagger in the heart of your love. If you tend to be a gripe collector, practice daily forgiveness by reiterating this phrase popularized by the father of rational-emotive behavior therapy, Dr. Albert Ellis: "We are all just fallible human beings and mistake-making machines" who need to be forgiven for our imperfections and transgressions. Or you may not be aware of your resentment toward your partner because you are subconsciously repressing it for fear of conflict. Ask yourself—am I feeling disconnected, dejected, or deserted by my partner?

We call these three escalating D's of disconnection, dejection, and desertion to be the demons of relationship demise. If you are plagued by these feelings, then you need to confront the source of these demons and find the strength to discuss your feelings with your partner. Reducing negative emotions will allow you to get back some of that happy, unencumbered passion you had at the beginning of your relationship. When issues are not addressed, they will fester, ruining whatever is left of your desire for each other. If you have a lot of serious unresolved issues with your partner, especially those dealing with money, in-laws, child-rearing, or chronic infidelity, see a marital therapist to help you solve them. If your partner is not interested in seeing a couples therapist with you, see one yourself for individual therapy, preferably with a cognitive-behavioral practitioner, even if you feel that your partner is the one "at fault."

While you may not be able to resolve the relational issues, you may feel less angry and resentful through the process of cognitive restructuring, or learning to identify negative thoughts and actively rebut them.

GENERAL DISCONTENT

Feeling discontent with your life also acts as a barrier to passion. Discontent doesn't mean depression—if you suspect that you or your partner is depressed, you should seek professional help immediately. However, most of the time, clinical depression isn't the problem—chronic discontent is.

Discontent often comes from "upward comparisons"—comparing yourself with someone who is better off than you are. You may wish you had someone else's good fortune, good looks, status, or luck. The problem? Someone will always be younger, healthier, wealthier, prettier, sexier, and luckier than you are. Negatively comparing your partner with others is another way to create discontent and discord in your relationship.

If you want to feel happy, compare yourself with those less fortunate than you are—one-sixth of the world population, or one billion people, and 12 percent of Americans live below poverty level. Increasing your gratitude for the blessings in your life amplifies your happiness. Start a gratefulness journal. Keeping a record of what goes right helps you see your glass of life as half-full rather than half-empty. You can help rewire your brain to feel more optimistic by focusing on the positive. Simply writing about the good parts of your day is proven to boost your happiness by 25 percent. If you don't like to write, you can simply take a moment to appreciate all the good things in your life right now, such as a sunny day, good friends and family, and decent health.

Psychological research has shown that only about 10 percent of happiness depends on external circumstances and 90 percent on your internal world. You may not be able to change the external circumstances, but you can modify your internal world by working on your thinking. To put it another way: Stop complaining that roses have thorns and be thankful that thorns have roses.

GIVING HAPPINESS TO GET HAPPINESS

Boost your happiness by increasing your generosity. Although we may believe that getting makes us happy, research consistently shows that giving makes us happier. Giving doesn't have to entail huge sacrifices. Research reveals that doing five nice things in a day—such as holding the door for someone—enhances your frame of mind for an entire week. Doing these good deeds within a twenty-four-hour period packs a bigger punch in terms of uplifting your self-esteem than doling them out over several days. Psychologists call this feeling "the helper's high."

So, cultivate generosity of spirit. An extension of generous giving is also graciousness, or forgiving. When you forgive others for their misdoings, you set your mind free to trust and love again.

The happiness of both partners is critical for a passionate union, because your moods are contagious. One research study has shown that a 30 percent increase in one partner's happiness boosts that of the other, and a drop in the happiness of one is a major downer for the other. When you feel unhappy, you don't feel passionate about life or about sex. Sexual passion is a kernel contained inside your zest for life. Even when you're having a bad day, try to smile and act cheerful. Say "Great!" instead of "Fine" when someone asks you about your day. Be grateful, generous, and forgiving to those around you, particularly your partner, and you will be amazed how much more passionate you'll feel toward each other.

> **Sex Rx Rule:** *Happy people are horny people.*
> *Remember the three magic G's of happiness: gratitude, generosity (giving), and graciousness (forgiving).*

DAY 7

Today, work on acceptance and forgiveness. Focus on accepting your body and your relationship with your partner. Let go of critical evaluation, dissatisfaction, and resentment; appreciate yourself and your relationship. You've been in your own body and your current relationship for too long to continually criticize and dislike them. The process of fully accepting yourself and your partner will certainly not happen overnight, but today you will begin the journey.

1. **Take off your clothes and stand in front of the mirror. Look at yourself without criticizing or judging.** Say to yourself in a strong, affirmative voice, "I like myself just the way I am. I accept the 'imperfections' of my body and even find them attractive. I am not ashamed

of or embarrassed about my body—on the contrary, I am proud of how I look. I appreciate the _____ _____(strength, flexibility, voluptuousness, resilience, femininity, ruggedness, and so on) of my body. I am thankful for everything my body can do for me. I can see why my partner is attracted to me." Jot down ten things you like about your appearance and keep the list handy for daily affirmations.

2. **Find your favorite photo of your partner.** Think of your most recent argument with your partner. Do you think the reason for your argument was important? Do you think it will still be important a month from now? What about a year from now? Imagine that your partner is gone and all you have left is this photo to remember him or her by. How would you feel if your partner were no longer alive? As you look at the photo, let all anger or resentment against your partner go and allow yourself to feel unconditional love. Look in your partner's eyes in the photo and tell your partner that you forgive him or her for everything. Thank your partner silently for being there for you all these years. Now tell this to your partner in person. Be as sentimental and melodramatic as you can, using phrases such as "I am so happy to have you in my life," "I can't imagine my life without you," or "You are the love of my life."

3. **Imagine that your relationship is a car.** When you perform caring, thoughtful, relationship-building acts, you put fuel in your gas tank. When you're selfish, insensitive, hurtful, and inconsiderate of your partner, you deplete the reserves of that tank. When the vehicle of your relationship is running on empty, it causes damage to its very engine—often irreparable damage. So visualize your Love Tank on a daily basis and think of different ways you can replenish the Love Fuel

in your Love Tank. What you do every day is more important than what you do once in a while.

It takes at least five positive relationship actions to offset one critical one, so make sure you always have extra credit in your Love Tank.

4. **Practice "peaking" while masturbating alone.** Engage in slow, sensuous self-pleasuring that doesn't have to end in orgasm. Practice delaying orgasm by peaking or coming close to orgasm, then allowing your arousal to subside. Try contracting your pelvic muscles (which you engage during daily Kegeling exercises) when you get close to orgasm. Peaking increases your ability to build up to a more powerful release.

   Research shows that many sexual dysfunctions can be resolved by changing your masturbatory style. Women can learn to experience greater pleasure during intercourse by pairing clitoral and vaginal stimulation, using fingers and/or sex toys, during masturbation. Men who get accustomed to fast, rough, and dry masturbatory practices often have difficulty reaching orgasm during intercourse because vaginal intercourse is wetter and softer than what they have conditioned themselves to. Adding lubricant and softening your touch during masturbation can recondition your orgasmic response. Men who ejaculate too quickly can train themselves to last longer by practicing peaking during masturbation.

5. **Perform sensate-focus exercises for ten minutes (five minutes each).** Concentrate on your partner's lower back and buttocks. Spice it up after a few minutes by experimenting with different types of touches—from very light and grazing to firm and probing. Try various massage techniques, from elongating your strokes and rolling the skin to lightly pinching, gliding, kneading,

hacking (using the edge of the palm in a flicking motion), and acupressure. But remember, do not succumb to the temptation to turn sensate focus into a sex romp. Reviving passion is a recipe that must be cooked slowly, with all the right ingredients added first—sampling it too early will result in a disappointing outcome! Afterwards, snuggle together and drift off to sleep remembering your List of Reasons and List of Turn-Ons and sharing them with each other.

DAY 7 SUMMARY

- Practice self-acceptance by using positive affirmations while standing in front of the mirror.
- Put your disagreements with your partner in perspective by fast-forwarding time and imagining how you will feel about them a few years from now.
- Think of your relationship as a car. The fuel tank is a repository of the thoughtful, kind things you do for each other—try to contribute to it daily.
- Perform sensate-focus exercises, concentrating on the lower-back and buttocks area.
- While engaging in self-pleasuring, practice peaking, or getting close to orgasm and then letting the arousal subside.

Insight for Her: Anger Dampens His Desire

Repressed anger or resentment is a frequent cause of low sexual desire in him. Often a man will blame his low libido on his health, fatigue, or work stress, when it is repressed anger and resentment toward you that causes his lack of sexual desire. His penis is connected to his heart; it's a barometer of his attachment, trust, and safety—even though many men are unaware of the connection. If he feels unappreciated, ignored, betrayed, or humiliated, his desire for you and his performance in bed may be impaired. Often, addressing and acknowledging the validity of his feelings will enhance his passion for you.

DAY 8

Today, continue to break down those emotional barriers to mutual passion and sexual fulfillment. Decrease resentment, guilt, and blame, and increase positive, happy, playful interaction. Meanwhile, do not forget your daily Kegeling and physical exercise, alone and together with your partner.

1. **Make a list of complaints about your partner's behavior.** Avoid generalized labels such as "a neat freak," personality traits such as "shyness," or character attacks. Include only those behaviors that occur on a regular basis and cause you to get irritated and upset with your partner, such as smoking in the house or not offering to do the dishes. Rate them on a scale of 1 to 10, with 1 being barely irritating and 10 being unbearably irritating. Choose the top five most irritating ones. Now phrase the behavior in this format: "When you do [name the behavior], I feel [name the emotion—sad, disappointed, angry, or whatever you feel]."

   Share the statements with your partner. Begin by saying, "Here are a few of your behaviors that I don't really like. Do you think you can change at least one of them if I reciprocate?"

2. **Take the sheet of paper with the list of complaints from the exercise above and rip it—or burn, shred,**

or pulverize it—whatever is most symbolic of letting go for you. This symbolic act represents forgiving your partner, giving your partner another chance to grow and change, and giving your partner the freedom to be as he or she is.

3. **Now write down ten ways your partner makes you happy.** These don't have to be regularly occurring behaviors, but ones you would like your partner to do more often, such as bringing flowers or offering a massage. State it in the following format: "I love it when you [name the behavior]." Call this Our List of Happy Ways. Share it with your partner and prominently display it in your office or on your refrigerator.

4. **Keep a journal entitled Our Happiness Diary.** Use this diary to record thoughts about your relationship, noting all sorts of interactions, but always ending with and elaborating on the positive ones. Research shows that when one partner commits his or her thoughts about the relationship to paper, the chances the couple will stick together increase by 20 percent. Twenty minutes a few times a week is sufficient to reap the relationship-boosting benefits of journaling. You don't have to share your outpourings with your partner—the journaling act itself helps you process your thoughts and clarify your feelings. Keep the descriptions of relational gripes to a minimum and elaborate on the happy interactions with your loved one.

5. **Perform sensate-focus exercises for ten minutes.** Today you can spice things up a bit. This time wear less clothing—you can do it in your undergarments (bra and panties for the female partner, underwear for the male partner). You can begin by touching your partner's neck, back, and legs, then turn your partner over and massage his or her stomach (but still stay away from breasts and

genital areas). Keep caressing very slowly and direct all your attention to where you touch your partner's skin. The receiver should focus entirely on where his or her partner is touching him or her. Now you can add your favorite massage oil and make your strokes more sensuous and suggestive. Feel the difference between relaxing sensate-focus massage and sensuous touch? You and your partner will probably get turned on now, but remember—no sexual intercourse yet.

6. **Engage in side-by-side self-pleasuring.** You have probably gotten turned on from your partner's sexual touch and are now craving release. You can have it—by self-pleasuring together. You don't have to talk tonight. Simply watch your partner masturbate, observing how your partner likes to do it. Make mental notes. Later, you can jot them down in a His and Hers Pleasure Manual.

DAY 8 SUMMARY

- List your complaints regarding your partner's behavior. Ask your partner to trade one important change for one you agree to make. Destroy the rest of the list to symbolize your forgiveness of your partner's faults.
- Write down ten ways your partner makes you happy and share it with him or her.
- Keep a relationship happiness diary by jotting down happy interactions you've enjoyed with your partner at least a few times per week.
- Perform sensate-focus massage for ten minutes, this time in your undergarments.
- Engage in side-by-side self-pleasuring and make notes for your His and Hers Pleasure Manual.

Insight for Him and Her: Venting Your Anger Is Not Cathartic

Although you may be tempted to go off on your partner, venting your anger won't make you feel better. Expressing anger aggressively amplifies it, whereas abstaining from confrontation dissipates it. However, you don't want to repress your feelings entirely. Avoiding conflicts altogether has been shown to cause negative health effects in the long term.

Wait for your anger to dissipate and then share your complaint with your partner. State only one complaint at a time in a calm, low voice; avoid personal attacks and bringing in past grievances. State your complaint this way: "I feel [name the emotion] when you do [name the behavior]." It's okay to argue, as long as you fight fair.

Insight for Him: Affirm Her Attractiveness

When a woman doesn't feel sexy, she's unlikely to be in the mood for sex. Be supportive of her efforts to stay fit and compliment her figure. No matter how many times you've told her that her body looks hot, she can never hear it enough. Our looks-obsessed culture makes even the most attractive women insecure about their bodies and in need of frequent affirmations of their attractiveness from the men they love.

CHAPTER 5

Enhancing Intimate Communication

Passion can exist without intimacy. You may have experienced earth-shattering passion during one-night stands and with partners about whom you knew little or to whom you felt little intimate connection. And intimacy doesn't necessarily create passion. You may have a warm and close friendship with someone for whom you have no sexual attraction or passion.

THE PASSION EQUATION

So if intimacy and passion aren't strongly connected, why is this chapter about improving your intimacy? Because great sex without intimacy is possible only in new and short-term relationships, when you're infatuated with your lover. As lust dims, novelty wears off, sexual attraction for each other diminishes, and intimacy becomes the fuel that fans lasting passion.

The desire for sexual encounters is chemically induced—in men and women, testosterone is responsible for sexual thoughts and fantasies, or what we call lust. This free-floating sexual desire becomes focused on a specific someone when you meet a person who fits your pre-existing template of desire, or love map. When that happens, your brain floods your body with neurotransmitters—adrenaline and dopamine—the exciting, feel-good hormones. No wonder you can't sleep or eat and feel high as a kite! You're full of natural stimulants and antidepressants.

But all good things come to an end, and so does this period of initial attraction and infatuation, called limerence. Once the reality sets in and you get to know each other on a daily basis, the idealization fueling limerence dissipates like morning fog.

LUST (testosterone) + LIMERENCE (adrenaline and dopamine) = GREAT PASSION

Inevitably, time and familiarity erode the novelty of your love affair, and you stop idealizing your lover. Once you stop idealizing your partner and see his or her true colors, you may feel you're falling out of love, that you no longer experience that chemistry.

At this point, many couples break up, and only those who have developed attachment-based intimacy will continue to enjoy each other's company.

Like limerence, attachment-based intimacy is fueled by chemicals in the brain. But attachment-based intimacy triggers the release of oxytocin and vasopressin, which create warm and fuzzy feelings when you're around your loved one. Attachment-based intimacy can form a solid foundation for a satisfying sex life as it gives a couple a sense of security, safety, connection, and bonding. You have to create solid relationship soil in which the seeds of your passion will grow and thrive.

LUST (testosterone) + INTIMACY (oxytocin and vasopressin) = GOOD PASSION

CREATING PASSION THROUGH INTIMACY

In long-term relationships, passion is not as effortless as it was initially. You have to create the right ambiance, treat your partner well, and make a conscious connection through intimate communication. The fire of your passion has to be kindled and maintained in order for it to burn as brightly as before. Highly erotic intimacy requires attention, affection, appreciation, affirmation, and admiration.

> **Sex Rx Rule:** *Remember the five A's of passionate intimacy—attention, affection, appreciation, affirmation, and admiration.*

PASSION PILLAR #1: ATTENTION

After your initial attraction wears off, you often stop paying attention to your lover. With the passage of time, your partner may become psychologically invisible to you. With so many distractions competing for your attention, your partner is often the last one you notice or attend to. We often give more attention to our friends than our partners. This process, called habituation, kills relationships.

The strength of your marriage rests on how readily you respond to a spouse's bid for attention. Do you continue to answer your e-mail when he walks through the door? Does he keep his eyes on the TV screen when answering you? When was the last time you sat down and had a tête-à-tête conversation?

Be excited when you see your partner after a long day of being apart and make sure to spend at least five minutes inquiring about his or her day. Notice changes about your partner's appearance (a new haircut or tie) and comment on them. Acknowledge your partner when he or she walks into the room. Turn off any electronics if your partner is attempting to get your attention, and always maintain eye contact during conversation. Be your partner's number one friend.

PASSION PILLAR #2: AFFECTION

Affection often gets forgotten in long-term relationships. Yet, research shows that people are 47 percent more likely to feel close to a family member who often expresses affection than to one who rarely does. Affection can be both verbal and nonverbal, such as handholding, hugging, and kissing. Some therapists suggest that warm contact such as hugs and handholding before the start of a long day has a lasting and protective benefit throughout the day. Humans of all ages thrive from affectionate touch. Don't be an affection withholder—dispense your affection to your partner often and generously. Be your partner's number one source of soothing comfort and warmth.

PASSION PILLAR #3: APPRECIATION

Feeling unvalued or unappreciated erodes your passion for your partner by breeding bitterness and resentment. It is the most frequent complaint we hear in couples therapy sessions. Partners who feel unappreciated by each other put less and less effort into the relationship—the same way an undervalued worker loses motivation to work hard and just goes through the motions.

Take time every day to account for all the things your partner does that contribute to your relationship—big and small, as it is often the small effort that gets overlooked the most. Does your partner go out of his way to stop at a coffee shop and get you a Frappuccino? Does she Tivo your favorite show or pick up your favorite paper? When you give your partner more appreciation, you will receive more in return. A relationship is like a mirror: It reflects the emotion you project on it. Be your partner's number one fan.

PASSION PILLAR #4: AFFIRMATION

To affirm your partner is to express your understanding of her goals and aspirations, to support his dreams and desires, and to assist in your partner's growth and self-actualization. Many people do not see the connection between lack of affirmation and lack of passion in their relationships. But how can you be passionate for someone who doesn't believe you can achieve your aspirations? Lack of affirmation breeds distance and estrangement.

Give your partner encouragement whenever you can and you will create an atmosphere of affirmation in your relationship. Tell your partner, "Don't give up. It's going to take a while, but you will get there" or "You are really getting the hang of it. I knew you could do it" or "We will get through this; you will see." When you affirm your partner, you are imbuing your relationship with faith and resilience, and your partner will reciprocate when you feel weak and need encouragement. Be your partner's number one supporter.

PASSION PILLAR #5: ADMIRATION/ADORATION

Attention, affection, affirmation, and appreciation lay the groundwork for intimacy, but to reach intense erotic intimacy, you need to add admiration and adoration to this formula. We feel our sexiest and most desirable when our partners admire and adore us, yet the more we get to know each other, the less admired and adored we feel.

Think of all the qualities you admire in your partner, such as a sense of humor, courage, perseverance, inquisitiveness, equanimity, magnanimity, or joie de vivre, and express your admiration for them often. Adoration is a more intense form of admiration—it is profound love, admiration, and loving devotion. Learning to express adoration for your all-too-familiar partner may feel a bit like swimming against the tide. Find all the little things you find adorable about your partner—his dimpled chin, her accent, the way she twirls her hair, his way of playing with the dog. Compliment your partner and tell your partner "I adore you" as often as you can. Try it in different languages: "*Je t'adore*" in French or "*Ti adoro, tesoro mio*" in Italian.

You can express your admiration or adoration for your partner with cards or other symbolic gifts or gestures. Tape a note to the computer screen, spray "I love you" with shaving cream on the bathroom mirror, record it in a voice-activated photo frame, or write it on the inside of the wrapper of her favorite candy or gum. Be your partner's number one admirer.

DAY 9

Today, begin to pay greater attention to your partner. Be more affectionate. Express appreciation for everything your partner does for you and for having your partner in your life. Don't forget to maintain previous commitments, such as exercising together, watching your nutrition, and Kegeling.

1. **Find five minutes of uninterrupted time and sit down across from your partner for a tête-à-tête.** Although face-to-face talk can be uncomfortable, even in long-term committed relationships, it's important to do it.

   Look at your partner as if for the first time. Don't focus on imperfections. Instead, admire him or her the way an artist would admire a painting. Notice all the things you like about your partner. Take two minutes to tell about your day. Now let your partner take a turn. Don't interrupt each other, but show you're listening.

2. **Write down five things you appreciate about your partner.** This could include making coffee in the morn-

ing, taking your clothes to the dry cleaners, and so on. Preface your list with "I know I don't always tell you how much I appreciate everything you do for me, and sometimes it may even seem like I don't notice or take it for granted. But I do appreciate everything you do, even when I forget to express it. Thank you for being so [name the behavior]. It's so nice when you [name the action]."

After you've completed your list, share it with your partner via e-mail, a letter, or a phone call. If you use a diary or an agenda, write down An Appreciation Thought related to your partner or your relationship and share it with your partner regularly.

3. **Give your partner *huggus uninterruptus*.** Make this type of embrace part of your passion-enhancing routine. When your partner walks through the door, instead of giving him or her a perfunctory hug, connect in a long embrace and don't break it off for a few minutes. As you hold your partner close to you, feel his heartbeat, hear her breathing, breathe in the aroma of her skin. Wait until your partner's body begins to feel relaxed and almost limp in your embrace. Research shows that when couples hug for twenty seconds, their levels of oxytocin increase dramatically. Those in loving relationships have the highest increases. *Huggus uninterruptus* is one of the easiest ways to express nonverbal affection for your partner on a daily basis.

4. **Practice a modified version of sensate-focus exercises.** Now, you'll focus on an exploration of the sensuous realm. This time, you and your partner will be active. Ask your partner where and how he or she likes to be touched the most, and when it's your turn, tell your partner what parts of your body feel particularly sensitive, sensuous, ticklish, receptive to stimulation. Try varying your stimulation from hard and probing to

light and sensuous. Avoid surprising your partner during this exercise. Instead, practice communication by telling your partner what you intend to do next. Barely graze your partner's skin, touching the hairs on his or her body instead of touching the skin. Touch your partner with different textures, such as silk, cashmere, and fur. Use different temperatures, such as grazing her body with a scarf warmed by a dryer or rolling a cold water bottle placed in a towel over his body.

5. **Engage in side-by-side self-pleasuring.** Tonight, you won't be a mere observer, you'll describe to your partner exactly how you like to be touched. Sit or lie down next to each other, but not so close that your bodies are touching. Take turns masturbating slowly, with peaking, and pay close attention to your partner when he or she is self-pleasuring. As you touch your body, tell your partner which areas feel particularly sensitive and what kind of touch feels particularly good. Be as specific as you can in your descriptions. When your partner describes how he or she likes to be touched, make sure to jot it down in the His and Her Pleasure Manual. You will later use this manual to create erotic stories and fantasies to ignite each other's erotic imagination. Close your eyes and imagine that it is your partner who is touching you. Imagine how wonderful it will feel when very soon you will make that fantasy a reality!

DAY 9 SUMMARY

- Spend five minutes of uninterrupted time talking tête-à-tête.
- List five things you appreciate about your partner and share the list with him or her.

- Give your partner a thirty-second *huggus uninterruptus*.
- Practice ten minutes of modified sensate-focus exercises during which you vary stimulation and report to your partner how and where you like to be touched.
- Engage in side-by-side self-pleasuring while sharing with your partner where and how you like to be touched and making notes for the His and Her Pleasure Manual.

Insight for Him and Her

DIFFERENCES BETWEEN HER AND HIS SEXUAL COMMUNICATION	
Women	**Men**
Relate through talking together	Relate through doing things together
Face-to-face communicators	Side-by-side communicators
Find relationship talk soothing	Find relationship talk confrontational
Assert themselves through questions	Assert themselves through direct demands
Want tête-à-tête prior to sex	Want sex prior to tête-à-tête

Insight for Her: Don't Make Him Face You

Don't push him for face-to-face conversation. Although women derive a great sense of satisfaction from heartfelt eye-to-eye confessions, men feel uncomfortable, and often threatened, by such direct disclosures. Men prefer to open up in side-by-side interactions, while they're working or playing alongside you. That's why engaging in athletic activities together can be so helpful in reviving a relationship.

Insight for Her: Express Admiration for Him

Many women think men don't need to be complimented as much as women do. Although most women seek affirmations of their femininity, men are just as needy when it comes to wanting affirmations of their masculinity—but they're much less likely to ask for them. Women are more responsive to praise about their physicality, while men appreciate being praised for character traits. Make sure to compliment his problem-solving skills, his tenacity at work, his way with children, his concern for the environment.

DAY 10

Today, continue enhancing your intimate and erotic communication with your partner by expressing your admiration and adoration. Come up with the terms of endearment that will become part of your everyday vocabulary. Feel each other's naked bodies and kiss for the first time in ten days!

1. **Write down ten things you admire or adore about your partner.** They can be physical, emotional, or spiritual; trivial or global; serious or funny or sexual. Begin your admiration sentences with "I admire." Begin your adoration sentences with "I adore." Elaborate on the reasons why you find a specific feature or behavior of your partner to be admirable or adorable. For example, maybe you admire your partner's ambition and persistence. Maybe you adore your partner's dimples or the shape of his or her hands. Now share the Admiration/ Adoration List with your partner.

2. **Exaggerate your admiration for your partner, even fib if you have to.** Honesty is an important foundation for trust in a relationship, but can be a bitter dish that is better served warm, in small doses, and with the right condiments.

   When it comes to judging your partner, it's better to overlook the occasional unsightly or negative characteristic, and adoration allows you to do that. When your partner asks you, "Do you think my bald spot is really noticeable?" it's okay to fib and say, "It's not so bad. I adore you just as much with or without that little spot." Or when she inquiries whether her cellulite is obvious to you, go ahead and lie, "What cellulite? All I see is a sexy, voluptuous goddess."

   Think of other values that may trump the importance of honesty, such as compassion, loyalty, and encouragement. One person complained that her husband, who is actually a therapist, responded to her inquiry of "What can I get you for Christmas?" with "Nothing, the best present you can give me is to lose ten pounds." Needless to say, that kind of honesty was not beneficial to the relationship.

3. **Use terms of endearment when addressing your partner.** These terms can be playful or serious, already existing or made-up on the spot. Call him or her "honey," "sweetie," "darling," "beloved," or "my love"; or go for foreign language terms such as *"ma cherie," "mi tesoro,"* or *"moi lybimyi."* Use your partner's name in the same sentence, such as "Philip, my honey" or "Mary, my love." Research has shown that people love to hear their names mentioned; it can trigger the pleasure hormones in our brains. You will notice that such communication, although it may feel sappy or artificial at first, will actually endear your partner to you.

And your partner will probably respond with increased expressions of tenderness toward you.

4. **Perform sensual touching exercises for ten minutes (five minutes each).** Tonight, apply the lessons you learned from sensate-focus touch, but practice sensuous touching instead. Get totally undressed. This time you can touch with intent to arouse and no place on the body is off-limits. The passive partner shouldn't respond in any way, just enjoy being touched. You can vary your touch to see what your partner likes most— light pinching motion between thumb and forefinger is best used along either side of the spine, from the top of the neck to the tailbone at the top of the buttocks. Long, gliding strokes under the shoulder blades and along the rib lines and down the spine are sensuous. At the buttocks, you can use a harder kneading motion. You and your partner will probably get aroused doing this exercise—acknowledge this arousal, but do resist the urge to do anything about it. Let it subside.

5. **Snuggle with your partner in bed after you are finished with sensual touching.** Make sure you're free of all distractions. Turn toward your partner, gaze into each other's eyes, then slowly lean over and kiss for the first time in ten days. Try to maintain the gaze, searching for the connection. Eyes-open kissing is an old Tantric technique that increases intimacy. Be mindful as you kiss. Engage all of your senses. Make the kiss as long and sensuous as you want, but don't go further. Through delayed sexual gratification, you can cultivate and grow your passion for each other. Build up the volcano of your desire to be released tomorrow.

DAY 10 SUMMARY

- Write down ten things you admire or adore about your partner, then share it with him or her.
- Exaggerate your adoration and admiration for your partner, even if you have to fib a little.
- Use terms of endearment such as "my love" and "*ma cherie*" when addressing your partner.
- Perform sensual touching exercises, slowly, the way you performed sensate focus.
- Give your partner a long, sensual, eyes-open, erotically charged kiss, but don't have sex yet.

Bonus Points for Him: Share Your Problems with Her

Instead of stoically dealing with a problem yourself, talk to her about what's on your mind and ask what she thinks. She'll feel involved, loved, and appreciated; you'll feel heard, and you just might get a great piece of advice on how to handle the problem.

She can be especially helpful if what's troubling you involves another woman, such as your mother, sister, or a coworker. Most important, you won't feel alone in dealing with the problem. Research shows that the most reliable predictor of not being lonely for both genders is the amount of communication you have with women. Talking to your buddies won't make you feel any better. No wonder both men and women prefer to gossip with other women. Women have a lot of empathy for other people and tend to be better listeners than men—so give her a chance to hear you.

CHAPTER 6

Revealing Sexual Vulnerability

Now that you've removed major emotional barriers and improved your intimate communication, it's time to dig deeper, to find the roots and undercurrents of your sexual desire. Your sexual thoughts, preferences, and fantasies are shaped by your love map, or mental blueprint of your desire, usually formed in early childhood. Often, these beliefs were formed when you were too small to even understand the concept of sexual desire, so you may not have any cognitive memories of how they came about. The way your caretakers touched or punished you, the associations you formed between pleasure, security, and the people you liked have all shaped your love map. Each person's desire blueprint is unique.

HOW YOUR DESIRE BLUEPRINT WORKS

You don't always realize your desire blueprint's effect on you until something goes wrong. Bob, for example, lost desire for his wife about the same time she cut off her long blond hair. After some encouragement, he recalled his interactions with his early caregivers. It turned out that one of his favorite aunts—who visited seldom but was always attentive and loving—used to brush her long, blond hair 100 strokes before going to bed (a practice popular at that time). As she did this, she recounted elaborate fairy tales to little Bob, who cuddled next to her in bed.

Her long hair became associated with warmth, attention, and affection for Bob, as its silkiness became imbued with magical qualities invoked through the narrative of her fairy tales.

No wonder his wife's haircut triggered such instantaneous aversion in him—the magic of his arousal was wrapped into her long hair. Relating this story to his spouse was a turning point for salvaging their defunct sex life—she agreed to grow her hair out and get temporary hair extensions.

FORMATIVE FIRSTS AND PEAK SEXUAL MEMORIES

Your sexual preferences and fantasies are further formed by so-called "formative firsts" and "peak sexual memories," which constitute the next two layers of erotic associations. Your first erotic encounters, such as the first time you held hands, kissed, and had oral sex and intercourse, formed lasting impressions—your formative firsts. You may have tried oral sex early and found it to be gross, which is always in the back of your mind now. Or, you may have found kissing to be particularly exquisite because it felt so grown-up and affectionate, and you miss it now when your partner makes it brief and perfunctory.

The next crucial layer of your sexual history holds your most moving sexual experiences. These peak sexual memories shape your daily sexual fantasies. If you liked the boy who pulled your ponytail in grade school, and your first lover was dominant and forceful, your fantasies may include being manhandled by a strong yet sensitive brute.

Learning to tap into the fertile soil of each other's fantasy land is the surest way for a couple to find the geysers of their secret passions. Exploring your own fantasies and selectively sharing them with your partner will be one of the most important ways to keep your passion alive.

Sex Rx Rule: Desire Blueprints + Formative Firsts + Peak Sexual Experiences = Sexual Fantasies

HEADING FOR FANTASY ISLAND

Fantasy is the fabric of our lives. We fantasize about Hollywood fame, *Fortune* 500 wealth, presidential power, pageant beauty, athletic prowess, long-lasting health, and the return of our lost youth, but our most frequent, vivid, and persistent fantasies are the ones about sex. Sexual fantasies are evoked by our favorite songs. They surreptitiously lurk behind seductive magazine ads, creep into our consciousness during romantic movie scenes, and boldly glare at us from the pages of adult magazines and romance novels. Sexual fantasy prolongs the pleasure of the past sexual encounter, amplifies enjoyment of the present one, and foreshadows upcoming passions. Sexual fantasy can sustain your sexuality during times of romantic drought. It can reawaken lost desire and save stale relationships.

Both men and women engage in sexual fantasy. Research shows that more than 95 percent of men and women have experienced a sexual fantasy in their lives. According to one study, 91 percent of the women questioned regularly engaged in sexual fantasy to increase their sexual arousal.

Fantasies can be provoked by external stimuli or generated internally. Externally triggered fantasies arise when you see visually exciting material, such as a photo of an attractive person, or receive auditory stimulation, such as your favorite song. Men appear to have twice as many externally generated fantasies as women. This is probably due to men's visual orientation. Fantasies have been shown to be associated with high libido (as defined by high sex drive) and orgasm frequency. This is especially true for women: Those who had more sexual fantasies also had higher sexual desire and sexual satisfaction.

Fantasy can break through the barriers to arousal, such as distraction, conflict, or boredom with your partner. It can transport you to a more erotic setting, transform your view of yourself, and even imbue your partner with imaginary characteristics he or she lacks.

COMMON FANTASY THEMES

When it comes to fantasy content, the majority of men and women prefer similar fantasy themes. One of the pioneering studies of fantasy found that the following five fantasies are most common for both men and women:

1. Sex with a loved one
2. Sex with a stranger
3. Sex with multiple partners of the opposite sex at the same time
4. Doing things sexually that you would never do in reality
5. Being forced or forcing someone to have sex

Intercourse with a loved partner was found to be the most exciting fantasy for both men and women in this study. But don't worry if your fantasies don't always involve your partner. Two other studies found that the two most popular fantasies for both men and women were being with another partner and reliving a previous sexual experience.

Common Sexual Fantasies—Explained

- **Sex in an exotic location.** No matter how nice your bedroom is, you may get turned on by having sex in different places, such as the beach or a meadow.
- **Sex with a former lover.** Although you may occasionally recall doing it with an ex, it doesn't mean you want to get back together with him or her, so no need to worry.
- **Sex with someone else you know.** You might find yourself fantasizing about your boss or coworker in the next cubicle, or even your best friend or neighbor.
- **Sex in public.** You may fantasize about public sex, such as doing it on the balcony while others are watching. Women are slightly more likely to enjoy the thought of public sex than men.
- **Sex with a stranger.** Men aren't the only ones who enjoy the thought of noncommittal sex. Women, too, fantasize about a wild tryst with a handsome stranger they will never see again.
- **Nonconsensual sex.** Forcing or being forced into having sex is a common fantasy for men and women. She dreams of a sensitive, caring brute who will find her so irresistible that he will be overwhelmed with an urgent desire to take her, using just the right amount of force to overcome her token resistance. He imagines being tied up by a strong and gorgeous Amazon who ruthlessly uses him for her sexual pleasure.
- **Bi-curious fantasies.** Although the majority of women have bi-curious fantasies, many men also fantasize about same-sex experimentation. Having such fantasies does not make you gay.
- **Sex with a celebrity.** Men usually find plenty of stimulating eye candy on TV, whereas women love perusing

gossip magazines, which gives them plenty of fantasy material.

- **Sex with multiple partners.** The harem is a favorite male fantasy. Women also enjoy the thought of being satisfied by multiple sexual partners at once.

Although the studies found that men and women fantasize about similar sexual themes, the style of their fantasies is dramatically different. Women's fantasies are more emotional, contextual, intimate, and romantic. Unlike men, women rely less on vision and more on thinking and emotional processes in their sexual fantasies. Women's fantasies have more references to affection and commitment. Men, on the other hand, are more likely to fantasize about specific sexual acts and visualize physical parts of the bodies. Even though the women's fantasies are just as vivid, they are frequently unable to provide the same descriptive details about the objects of their fantasies.

Instead, women appear to be involved more with their own emotional responses and characteristics than with the characteristics of their imaginary partners. Their fantasies frequently include descriptions of their imagined selves, such as "I look so sexy wearing my favorite blue lingerie and he can't take his eyes off me." Women are also more likely to describe feelings that their fantasies evoke: "I felt happy and free."

DIFFERENCES BETWEEN HIS AND HER FANTASIES	
Female	**Male**
Less frequent	More frequent
Contextual	Visual
Passive	Active
Intimate	Promiscuous
Focus on emotions	Focus on acts and body parts

FEELING GUILTY AND ASHAMED OF SEXUAL FANTASIES

Women are more likely than men to feel conflicted about their sexual fantasies. About one in four people feels strong guilt about their fantasies. Most people feel guilty fantasizing while making love to their partner because they consider such fantasies a form of symbolic betrayal or cognitive infidelity.

Having sexual fantasies about someone other than your partner may make you question your integrity—how can you be in love with one person and think about another? The way most people deal with this form of guilt is to repress it. In one study of college students, 22 percent of women and 8 percent of men said they usually try to repress the feelings associated with fantasy. People also feel guilty when their fantasies and personal ideologies are in conflict. A strong and independent woman may feel guilty and ashamed about having fantasies of being dominated by an insensitive brute.

People who have what they consider to be unusual or deviant fantasies may also feel guilt and shame about them—and may even fear that such fantasies will cause them to lose control or act out in socially unacceptable ways. Research has shown that those who feel guilty about their fantasies have sex less often and enjoy it considerably less. If you feel guilty about your fantasies, recognize them as normal. If you think your partner feels shameful or guilty about his or her fantasies, you can try to help by normalizing these fantasies and encouraging your partner to accept them. Get your partner an erotic book and talk about your fantasies.

One client, a shy woman raised in a conservative Catholic environment, told us, "I never felt comfortable about sharing my submission fantasies until my husband got me *Story of O* (an acclaimed French novel about female submission, written by Pauline Reage). After reading it, I feel much more comfortable about my fantasies and have even enacted some of them with my husband."

REALITY VERSUS FANTASY

A widespread belief holds that many women fantasize about being raped and, thus, want to be raped. This belief is fueled by reports of female-submission fantasies. It's true that many women have fantasies of being overpowered and taken against their will. However, the erotic fantasy of "rape" is much different from the reality of rape.

When a woman fantasizes about being raped, she imagines a sexually desirable man, motivated by passion that her sexual attractiveness arouses in him, who uses just enough force to overcome her resistance and to promote her pleasure. In reality, rape is not sexual but violent in its motivation and execution. The world of difference between rape fantasy and rape can be expressed in one word: control. Descriptions of rape fantasies that women find arousing often emphasize the man's desire for the woman, his efforts to arouse her passion, and the woman's token resistance eventually giving way to her participation. Throughout the rape fantasy, the woman feels subjectively in control, permitting the man to "rape" her for her own erotic gratification.

"Fantasizing about being taken by a handsome stranger is one of my favorite fantasies," admitted one client. "One time I was swimming laps at our community pool next to this really hot guy, and I kept on imagining how he would grab me, drag me into the bushes, and have his way with me for a couple of sinful hours," she laughed. "I felt so guilty about these thoughts."

SHARING SEXUAL FANTASIES

Many people wonder how to go about sharing their hidden sexual fantasies or how to get their partner to open up about his or her fantasies. If you want to share your sexual fantasies with your lover and get to know his or hers, you need to proceed cautiously. Sharing sexual fantasies with your partner requires good communication and a high degree of trust. One way you can do it without risking your partner's revulsion or feeling too vulnerable is by renting a mainstream movie or DVD involving sexual fantasies and then discussing it together.

For example, the TV show *Nip/Tuck* features just about every taboo fantasy, including bondage and discipline, sex with a transvestite, partner pretending to be a prostitute. *Bitter Moon,* a Roman Polanski movie, shows a couple engaging in steamy acts of mild S&M, voyeurism, and exhibitionism; *Wild Things* portrays a hot threesome with Denise Richards.

Encouraging your partner to trade fantasies is another way to bring it up. Playing an adult version of Truth or Dare and other games requiring disclosure is a playful way to approach such disclosure.

Talking about Fantasies

Talk with your partner about his or her sexual fantasies. Ask these questions:

- What are the settings and ambiance of your fantasies?
- Are there multiple partners involved? Are they familiar lovers or novel and strange?
- Is there an element of surprise? Is your sexuality being put on display? Are you being watched while you are engaging in sexual acts or do you put on a show?
- In your fantasies, do you fantasize "doing" your sex partner or "being done"? Are you the center of attention or are you there to pleasure another?
- Are you a willing participant or are you being overpowered and forced into sex?

- How much resistance do you imagine employing: Are you easily overpowered or do you put up a screaming, kicking fight?
- Do you enjoy an eloquent, articulate master or a quiet one who says little other than barking orders?
- Do you want your master to express physical attention and affection or to be distant and aloof?
- Do you get turned on imagining serving your master by performing various tasks or by simply becoming an inanimate object of sexual gratification?
- How much erotic corporal punishment do you imagine receiving in your fantasies? Does adding pain to sexual sensations increase the pleasure you feel?

Never push your partner into fulfilling a fantasy. Instead, gently encourage him or her to further explore it. The first step in getting your lover to try out a fantasy is to normalize the experience—show your partner that it is not strange or abnormal to have this fantasy and that other people are prone to this fantasy as well. Reading books that compile women's fantasies, such as Nancy Friday's *My Secret Garden,* or going on the Internet to explore male fantasies on websites and chat groups together is a good first step in making the fantasy less frightening. In addition to watching mainstream films portraying sexual fantasies, consider watching couples-oriented X-rated films that further explore the particular fantasies.

Only when your partner expresses interest in fulfilling his or her fantasy should you begin to plan a way to carry it out. Keep in mind that fantasies often lose their erotic appeal after they're brought into practice, so if a fantasy is a particularly cherished one, it may be best left unfulfilled.

Sex Rx Rule: *Nothing revealed, nothing achieved.*

DAY 11

Today, begin to peel back each other's defensive layers to reveal glimpses of that secret sexual garden, the one replete with childhood yearnings, erotic dreams, forbidden fantasies, thrilling first-time experiences, and memories of the best sex you've had—in reality and in your fantasies. You can perform these recall exercises while Kegeling or while going for a brisk walk with your partner.

1. **Tap into your personal sexual history to try to figure out your love map, the desire blueprint of your libido.** Pull out your family albums and examine your childhood photos. What kinds of thoughts and feelings do the photos evoke—nostalgia, warmth, jealousy, relief at not being a kid anymore?

    How would you describe your parents—warm, distant, touchy-feely, sexually repressed, or emotionally unavailable? Did they hug you a lot? Were you allowed to sleep in your parents' bed when you were not feeling well? How did you feel when they kissed you—loved, smothered, detached, disgusted? Do you feel your needs for attachment and bonding were usually met or did you crave for your caretakers to hug and hold you more? Do you feel another sibling was favored over you and you had to compete for your parents' attention? Were there any other caregivers with whom you enjoyed spending time?

    Jot down any connections or associations you can think of. Although you may think your early childhood experiences have little bearing on your passion now, analyzing the origin of your desire is an important (albeit not the most pleasant) task for understanding your emotional dynamics with your partner and the barriers to your arousal.

2. **Take a walk down memory lane by recalling and writing down your romantic formative firsts.** Try to recall the first time you developed a childhood crush on a playmate or classmate. What was the object of your affection like? When was the first time you held hands, kissed, fondled, had oral sex, intercourse? Mentally rate each experience on a scale of 1 to 10. Think of what made some of those experiences magical and what made others not.

   Was there one particularly memorable experience that you would like to share with your partner? Was there a negative one that impacted how you view that sexual activity? Was there something you tried with your ex-partner that you wish you could try again in your current relationship?

   You don't have to share the full experience with your partner, as it may incite excessive jealousy and insecurity, unless you feel that giving your partner a glimpse would make him or her better understand your sexual needs. Write down all the ideas this exercise generated in the His and Her Pleasure Manual under the heading Things to Try. During this exercise you may recall how much fun it was to engage in fondling through clothes or dry-humping—something you may enjoy doing again.

3. **Write down your peak sexual experience with your partner.** Each of you should write down your own story as you recall it, without peeking to see what your partner is describing. For many couples, different events have different peaks. You may recall making love at a fabulous villa during an exotic getaway,

whereas your partner may remember the first time you made love in your new home.

After you've finished writing, make sure you have a distraction-free environment. Then snuggle comfortably in each other's arms and read your accounts of your peak sexual experiences to each other. After reading your accounts, close your eyes and recall each experience again, this time together, as you try to recreate it in your mind.

4. **Engage in mutual masturbation tonight while recalling your chosen peak sexual experience together.** One partner can recall an entire experience, or you can take turns recounting it and playing with each other. Attempt to involve as many of your senses as you can—feel the softness of your partner's skin, smell his cologne, hear her moans. Make sure you tell your partner what feels good and give plenty of feedback about how you like to be touched. Remember, what the mind perceives, the mind believes!

DAY 11 SUMMARY

- Try to figure out the erotic beginnings of your desire blueprint.
- Recall, rate, and write down your erotic formative firsts, such as your first kiss.
- Write down your peak sexual experience with your partner and share it with him or her.
- Go for a brisk walk and recall your peak experiences again.
- Engage in side-by-side mutual masturbation while recalling your peak sexual experiences together.

Insight for Him: She Has a Rich Fantasy Life

It may be hard to imagine that your busy partner has an abundant inner well of sexual fantasies, but chances are, she does—no matter how religious or conservative she may be. For centuries, it was an established truism that normal women don't experience sexual thoughts or fantasies, and even Freud opined that women don't have sexual fantasies. These myths about her lack of sex drive continue to be perpetuated into the present time, despite research that shows women can be as sexual as men, under the right conditions. If you want a glimpse into female fantasies, read Nancy Friday's compendium of women's fantasies, *My Secret Garden*.

DAY 12

Today, continue to tap into your secret erotic reservoir, diving deeper. Decide which fantasies you want to try out with your partner, write them down, and put them in the Jar of Our Desires from which you will draw on a weekly basis after you finish the Sex Rx Program. Choose one fantasy that your partner will help you bring to life during fantasy-guided masturbation tonight.

1. **Tap into your secret sexual fantasies and verbalize them.** Have you always dreamed of having sex in a convertible or trying a threesome or getting anal stimulation? Maybe you always wondered what it would be like to be tied up or spanked? Drop any shame you may have about the fantasy and let it out of the closet of your mind.

Look over the list of fantasy themes in the sidebar Common Sexual Fantasies—Explained. Decide which ones you want to keep as your secret turn-ons and which ones you want to share with your partner. Remember, sharing your fantasy will encourage your partner to open up as well, and maybe even to try it out! But it may also reduce the erotic appeal of the fantasy, so keep your most coveted ones to yourself (or reserve them to be shared later if you feel another lull in your mutual libidos).

Choose one fantasy such as "being overpowered by my partner and taken against my will" or "have my partner pretend she is my maid who is there to serve me" and elaborate on it in your mind.

2. **With your partner, go over the list of sexual fantasies you wish to explore.** Copy it and cut out the ones both of you are willing to try out and that don't require complicated planning. Put them in a basket or a jar. Label it Basket of Our Sexual Wishes or Jar of Our Desires. You can also add some of the ideas and fantasies you have been collecting in your His and Her Pleasure Journal. Put the basket or jar next to your bed and keep adding to it by coming up with your own naughty ideas. You'll take turns drawing from it once a week beginning on Day 19, when we address the naughtiness component of sizzling sex.

3. **Write down for your partner what you want him or her to do to you and how you like to be pleasured, using the following statements:**

- "I like it when you touch my . . ."
- "I prefer when you . . . "
- "It really turns me on when you kiss my . . ."
- "I want you to . . ."

Now combine how you want your partner to treat you with your chosen fantasy from #1. For example, if your fantasy deals with domination, you might write down something like this: "When I fantasize about being a slave boy tonight, I want you to call me a sissy and to make me kneel in front of you as you slap my face with your hands and breasts. I like it when you rough me up a bit. I want you to pinch my nipples, but not too hard, and play with my cock, but don't let me come until I beg for mercy."

4. **Engage in fantasy-guided mutual masturbation tonight.** Share your chosen fantasy with your partner by giving him or her the notes you took throughout the day. Your partner should either fulfill the fantasy while pleasuring you or describe the fantasy to you while masturbating you, depending on the type of fantasy material.

   For example, if she expressed a desire to be overpowered by two men on a deserted island, he should have her lie back and close her eyes as he describes to her the fantasy while pleasuring her: "You are lounging on a beautiful beach, topless waiting for your girlfriend to arrive. The sun feels hot on your body and you are totally relaxed. Suddenly you hear a loud noise and you see two strong local guys appear on the beach. They have dreadlocks and their muscular bodies . . ."

   If the fantasy involves the partner doing specific acts, such as anal penetration, then add anal stimulation while masturbating your partner and describing what you are doing to him or her.

DAY 12 SUMMARY

- Explore different sexual fantasies in your mind and choose one to share with your partner later tonight.

- Make a list of sexual fantasies and acts, and then cut out the ones you want to fulfill with your partner and put them in your Jar of Our Desires.
- Engage in fantasy-guided masturbation during which your partner retells to you your fantasy while touching you and masturbating you according to your instructions.

Insight for Him: Sex Carries Greater Emotional Meaning for Her

For evolutionary and economic reasons, women have traditionally linked sex with love because it strengthened their relationships and increased their sense of safety and security for themselves and their children. Fear of abandonment and the need for safety underlie the adage "Women trade sex for love." Although modern women rely less on men to provide for them financially and physically, intimacy and emotional connection are still more of a prerequisite for them than for men.

Insight for Her: Love Your Vulva

Some women are self-conscious about the appearance of their vulva, considering their genitals to be unattractive—too dark, too big, or too uneven. If you're uncomfortable with the look of your genitals, get the book called *Femalia*, by Joani Blank, which features close-up photos of female genitals of women of all ages and ethnic backgrounds. Seeing the variety and splendor of womanhood will make you feel better about the look of your own genitals.

PART 3

THE NOVELTY FACTOR: DAYS 13–18

CHAPTER 7

Reinventing Yourself

Who doesn't love the thrill of novelty—whether it's putting on a freshly purchased dress, taking a newly acquired car for a spin, or going out on a date with a new love interest? Our brains are stimulated by the surprise of novelty, making the passage of time seem slower and the emotional experience richer. New things trigger the production of feel-good dopamine, the natural high that shopaholics (and sexaholics) become addicted to. As the object or experience becomes old and familiar, our brains slow down the production of feel-good neurotransmitters.

WHEN NOVELTY WEARS OFF

Unfortunately, the novelty wears off of relationships just as it does dresses and cars. Familiarity leads to comfort, which kills sexual passion. As Honoré de Balzac put it, "Marriage must incessantly contend with a monster that devours: familiarity."

The ultimate irony of romance is that the "happily ever after" all romantics strive for is often the very enemy of the storybook romance. Passion, or limerence, is predicated upon novelty, uncertainty, longing—as soon as we happily possess "the limerent object" (as psychologists call your crush), it quickly loses its lustful luster. The prince's white horse disappears, his castle turns out to have been a chimera, and he slowly morphs into a burping, snoring frog—the fairy tales have it all backwards. The practice of having separate bedrooms (so common among royalty in medieval times) was probably the best idea for maintaining novelty and preserving the inevitable erosion of passion by familiarity.

| CHARACTERISTICS OF ROUTINE VERSUS NOVEL EXPERIENCE ||
Routine	Novel
Comfortable	Unpredictable
Regimented	Spontaneous
Boring	Exciting
= Boredom	= Passion

BRINGING THE NEWNESS BACK

What can be done to battle this passion-draining pull of familiarity? You have three options:

1. A new partner
2. A new life
3. A new you

All of the advice can be summed up in one word: change. Nature has programmed our sexuality to respond to novelty because a greater variety of sexual partners meant a greater variety of genetic permutations, and thus the best likelihood of survival of the species. Throughout the centuries of evolution, those who sought the most genetic variation for their offspring passed on the greatest variety of genes. This survival instinct programmed our modern brains to become bored and disinterested in the same sexual partner and to seek out new, unexplored sexual stimuli. Although we do not have to become victims of our evolutionary programming, we do have to work at keeping ourselves and our relationships novel and exciting, and to inspire our partners to remain continually interested in us.

Monogamy quickly turns into monotony in most coupled relationships, surrendering them to the stagnation of sexual ennui. Once passion no longer feels spontaneous and effortless, and good sex requires planning and effort, many people believe they have fallen out of love and are tempted to search for novel excitement. Most of those tempted will choose the easy route: finding new erotic stimulation by having an affair or leaving an old partner for a new one. And for a while the new partner sparks new passion. But the cycle will inevitably repeat itself. Most research shows that second and third marriages are even less stable than first ones.

If you want to remain passionately monogamous, you need to fool your brain into experiencing the subjective excitement of a novel stimuli with your current partner through growth and rediscovery. The challenge of the new and unexpected makes you grow and gives you a sense of satisfaction; it makes you passionate about life and stimulates your partner's sexual interest in you. By growing and changing, by adding other dimensions and revealing new layers, you can keep your partner continually intrigued and erotically charged.

Some couples are afraid that growing will make them grow apart—and there is always a risk that change will create tension or a rift between a couple, especially if one partner feels threatened by the growth of the other or is reluctant to make the effort to change as well. But it is a risk worth taking, for its alternative—stagnation—is the stultifying stranglehold of passion.

Add sexual novelty to your relationship by exploring your layers of eroticism—and your partner's. Many of them are like buds on winter trees—ready to bloom as soon as someone shines light and warmth upon them.

DAY 13

Today, work on creating the new, exciting you. Of course, you have already begun the process of reinvention by changing your lifestyle, engaging in more physical activity, exercising your pelvic muscles, being mindful and relaxed, and treating your partner with more admiration and adoration. Now it's time to take a deeper plunge into the sea of growth and change.

1. **Write down as many things as you can think of that you've always wanted to change about your appearance.** Have you ever wanted to grow a beard, pierce your belly button, or get a Brazilian wax? Don't show the list to your partner, as you want the changes to be a surprise. Divide these potential changes in two columns: changes you can make immediately, such as coloring your hair, and those that would take a while, such as losing weight.

   Now pick ten things you are actually willing to change. These changes can be major, such as getting a new haircut and color, or minor, such as choosing a new perfume. Make several short-term changes immediately, and put together a plan for reaching at least one of the long-term goals. If you're cautious about change, make a temporary one before committing to a permanent change, such as getting a henna tattoo or a semipermanent hair color. Acquiring new clothes, lingerie, or shoes—particularly something outside of your usual style—is an easy way for a woman to surprise and delight her partner.

2. **Take up a sexy hobby—alone or together.** By adding a new dimension to your character, you will become more interesting and intriguing to your partner. Try ballroom dancing or karate classes, horseback or

motorcycle riding. Sign up to test and write reviews of sex products. Start an erotic book–review club online or enroll in a photography course and practice boudoir photography on your friends. Take a drawing or sculpting class, or learn a foreign language. Nothing is sexier than being able to whisper naughty words to your partner in multiple languages: *"Baise-moi, cheri!"* *"Bums mich schneller, liebling!"* *"Chiavami, tesoro!"* *"Pozelyi menya!"*

Try belly dancing or surfing. Install a stripper pole in your bedroom and take striptease classes. Make a list of hobbies you'd like to try alone or with your partner and share your individual lists with each other.

3. **Choose a new sexy scent.** Use it only during your date nights. If you use it consistently and exclusively for your date nights, your partner will associate it with your sexy side and whenever the scent is present, it will trigger your partner's desire. It will also become a signal for you to abandon your tired, mundane self and awaken your alive, adventuresome self the minute you put it on.

Choose a scent you not only like, but one with a name that sounds erotic as well, such as Obsession or Sexy or Dior's Addict or Yves Saint Laurent's La Nuit De L'Homme. Do you like the spokesperson for the perfume or cologne? If you like Naomi Campbell, you will get in a sexier mood wearing her scent, Seductive Elixir. You might want to collect miniperfumes and use them to evoke certain moods: Outspoken by Fergie when you want to be daring; Extraordinary by Avon when you want to feel special; Very Sexy Now by Victoria's Secret when you want to feel desired.

Certain aromas have been known to stimulate libido since the times of the *Kama Sutra.* Our sense of smell stimulates the nerve endings of the olfactory bulb located at the back of the nose, which in turn stimulates a part of the brain called the limbic system that triggers our libido by signaling the pituitary gland—the master of the endocrine gland, which controls hormone production—to increase androgen production.

Take your time sampling scents, avoid sales pressure, and decide for yourself what scent and label makes you feel the sexiest. Labels have a huge subliminal effect on us—in one study women felt smarter after using a pen with an MIT logo and more glam toting a Victoria's Secret shopping bag.

4. **Think of a sexy cultural or historical icon you would like to emulate.** It could be your favorite movie star, singer, or athlete. What is it about him or her that you find sexy? For many women Marilyn Monroe, Sophia Loren, Madonna, or Kim Kardashian is the archetype of unabashed sex appeal, whereas many men admire Elvis Presley, James Bond, or Brad Pitt. History is full of erotically charged characters: the sexually unabashed Cleopatra and the lady-charmer Casanova.

   Now think of that person as your alter ego. How would you act differently if you were that person? Would your posture be more upright? Would you walk with a seductive swagger? Would you speak with a sexy accent? Now try to be a bit like that person whenever you want to get yourself and your partner in a sexy mood.

5. **Make love to your partner in a different way tonight.** You don't have to come up with any different sexual acts. Tonight is about changing something about *you,* trying on the new sexual persona you have just invented. If

you're usually passive, initiate a sexual interlude; if you're usually the take-charge party, assume a passive role.

By pushing yourself outside your usual role, you can actually alter how you perceive the world and how your partner perceives you. One study showed that when a woman walked over to a potential date rather than waiting for a man to approach her, she found her target to be more attractive and felt more confident during the encounter. By playing mind games with yourself, you can actually change who you are—so force yourself to be bold tonight!

Many women report that they get aroused faster when they try on the sexually aggressive role with their man. And many men enjoy "being taken." Take the lead tonight by becoming the seductress. Undress your partner seductively, feeling him through his clothes. Unbutton his shirt, then put your hand in his pants pocket, feeling his penis through the fabric. Ask him in your best rendition of Mae West addressing Cary Grant, "Is that a pistol in your pocket or are you just pleased to see me?" Then have him watch as you perform a striptease for him. When he is seated, push him down and then straddle him. Be vocal—tell him how much he turns you on and what you plan on doing to him tonight. If he is usually the passive partner, reverse the roles and have him take an active lead.

DAY 13 SUMMARY

- Write down ten things you would like to change about your appearance and break them down into short-term and long-term goals.
- Make a list of sexy hobbies you would like to try alone or with your partner.
- Find a new sexy scent to wear exclusively on date nights.

- Choose a sexy cultural or historical icon to emulate and take on his or her qualities.
- Change the role you usually play in the bedroom; if you are usually passive, be aggressive tonight and vice versa.

Bonus for Him and Her: Make Yourself Edible

What you eat can influence the taste and smell of your sweat and genitals (and, if you're a man, your semen). In general, dairy products create the foulest-tasting fluids, whereas alkaline-based foods, such as meat and fish, produce a bitter, fishy taste. Garlic, onions, cabbage, broccoli, asparagus, and cauliflower have high sulfur content, which tastes bitter. Too much coffee and chemically processed liquors will also cause a bitter taste. Fruits and high-quality alcoholic drinks such as pricier wines, absinthe, brandy, cognac, gold rum, sake, vermouth, and whisky are good for a pleasant, sugary flavor.

To make yourself taste finger-licking good, drink lots of water and eat lots of fruits (such as pineapple, watermelon, papaya, and mango) as well as vegetables (such as tomatoes, carrots, and cucumbers.) Herbs such as parsley, celery, and cinnamon improve your smell and taste. When you're thinking of a BJ or going down on her, eat some cinnamon buns with pineapple juice!

Insight for Her: Cultivate a Sexy Body

A sexy body isn't necessarily a flab-free perfectly sculpted size six. The frail sixties model, Twiggy, and today's curvaceous plus-size model, Emma, are both sex goddesses, each in her own right. The ideal weight is the one at which you feel healthiest, most energetic, vibrant, and alive. Although sexy women don't obsess over their weight and size, they do know a sexy body is strong and healthy. They find ways to keep it moving; they take care of it and infuse it with sensuality and grace.

DAY 14

Today, continue to reinvent yourself and encourage your partner to do the same by initiating and fostering positive change. Learn unconditional self-acceptance, which will make you more confident and secure. Give yourself permission to shop for erotically charged clothing. Surprise your partner.

1. **Write down ten things you wish your partner would change about his appearance or his behavior, things you think would make you desire your partner more.** Obviously, be kind and adoring and proceed very cautiously so as not to offend your partner. Make sure the changes are realistic, specific, and minor, and that they don't concern something your partner considers to be central to his identity.

   For example, asking your partner to trim his nostril hairs, file his nails, or occasionally shave his genitals is okay, but asking him to get hair plugs or to start taking Rogaine is not. Asking her to color her gray roots, wear a black lace garter belt, or French manicure her toes and nails is okay, but asking her to get liposuction on her thighs or get a boob job is not.

   Sexual requests are also acceptable, such as asking your partner to deep-throat you, but don't expect your partner to automatically acquiesce to your request. Swap lists and see if you're willing to trade a few changes. For example, one client wanted his wife to get her extremely crooked teeth straightened, but she was reluctant to wear braces at her age (mid-forties). As they talked, it turned out that she wanted him to get rid of his "turkey waddle," and they agreed to do both things for each other.

2. **Learn unconditional self-acceptance.** When you reviewed the list of desirable changes presented by your partner, you probably realized there were some things you cannot or are not willing to change. You need to accept these realities and express that acceptance to your partner. Most of us judge ourselves, at least some of the time, according to the opinions of others— either those expressed or those we believe others hold. To the extent we do so, we surrender our independence of thought and action, and become dependent on others to sustain our self-esteem. A better solution is to tell yourself that no opinion but your own is really important to you; whether or not others see you as sexy, you believe you are and you accept yourself in your entirety.

Rational-behavioral therapists call this "an elegant solution," when you can accept yourself regardless of the external factors in your life. An example of an elegant solution statement would be "I don't care whether my previous boyfriend found me unattractive once I gained weight. There are plenty of men out there who will find me sexy, and most importantly, I see myself as sexy and desirable."

Make a list of these so-called elegant solution statements that relate to issues you are now working on. When you catch yourself negating, doubting, or berating yourself, read these statements over and over.

3. **Visualize yourself as a sexually desirable, confident person.** Even if you feel low on a particular day, it often helps to "fake it till you make it." Because moods often follow actions, try acting as if you are indeed fully confident about your sexual desirability. Even if you're feeling fat, bloated, and tired, flaunt your body to your partner instead of concealing it. Research shows that confidence in itself is very erotic. Acting that way may fool your brain into believing you are actually feeling confident. For example, research has shown that when you force yourself to smile, you actually begin to feel happier (this is known as the facial feedback hypothesis). Research has also found that when people are in a good mood, they are more creative, successful in problem-solving, and sexually desirable. To help your brain snap into confidence-mode, visualize yourself as a confident, happy, relaxed person who emanates erotic energy to the world.

4. **Shop for seductive garments.** A flattering new garment has a way of putting you in a sexually confident mood. This is particularly true for women. But most couples in long-term relationships trade sexy, trendy clothes for pragmatic, comfy ones. When was the last time you bought some sexy lingerie or tight Calvin Klein jeans? If you're like most people, you're probably schlepping around the house in old sweats and mismatched socks.

   Go shopping together and pick up some new sexy garments, preferably red ones. Bill Blass spoke the truth when he declared, "When in doubt, wear red." Research clearly shows that men find women to be far sexier when they're wearing red than when they're wearing garments of any other color. And, although research is less definitive regarding female color preference, women may also perceive men dressed in red as more passionate.

This preference seems to have evolutionary roots. The earliest-known Homo sapiens at the dawn of time used red ocher to decorate and adorn themselves. Red is the color of passion and sensuality, and it has been shown to stimulate a faster heartbeat and breathing rate. It is often used in restaurants as an appetite stimulant. Red has a life-affirming, positive association for most of us—after all, it's the color of your blood and your heart. Red is the color most commonly found in national flags. In Victoria's native language, Ukrainian, the word for red comes from the same root as the word for beautiful: "krasna." When you want to turn him on, be his "Lady in Red." If you want to excite her, wear a new red shirt.

5. **Surprise your partner.** Make a list of actions your partner would least expect from you, something that would require you to put yourself outside your comfort zone. Research shows that embracing new challenges makes you feel more fulfilled than sticking to sameness. Your list could include any of the following:

- Send him flowers with a sexy note
- Write her a card with a risqué poem
- Prepare her a candlelight dinner with aphrodisiacs
- Draw him a bubble bath and wash his genitals with a sponge
- Offer to shave his genital area, or shave yours in a heart shape
- Invite her to a male-review strip club and get her a lap dance
- Get her a spa gift certificate for a massage and a Brazilian wax

- Get a spray or a real tan with a heart-shaped tan mark using a sticker
- Surprise her with a henna tattoo design in a genital area
- Do a slow, sexy striptease for him followed by a lap dance
- Book a rent-for-an-hour hotel room and open the door in lingerie
- Order an adult magazine subscription, such as *Penthouse* or *Playgirl*
- Blindfold him, put earphones on him, and gag him with an apple, then kiss all over
- Wear a thong and peek-a-boo bra instead of your usual lingerie
- Put on a daring role-play outfit you would have never worn before
- Do a naked webcast or Skype with her while traveling
- Offer to videotape your love making, point-of-view-porn-style
- Perform a sex act you always considered repulsive

Write "surprise night" on your calendar so your partner knows a surprise is coming that night—but, of course, he or she will not know the nature of the surprise. The anticipation and curiosity will drive your partner wild. Alternate surprise nights with your partner every few weeks. Tonight will be your first surprise night, so one of you should choose one activity from the list you compiled and do it before or while making love to your partner tonight. In light of your new unconditional self-acceptance, you shouldn't worry whether your partner will think it is silly or out of your character. Your confident new you is not afraid to try out anything you're curious about.

DAY 14 SUMMARY

- Write down ten things you wish your partner would change about his or her appearance or behavior.
- Accept the things you think or know your partner dislikes about you that you don't want to change; practice unconditional self-acceptance.
- Visualize yourself as a confident and sexually desirable person and that's how you'll be perceived by others.
- Shop for new sexy, flattering, preferably red garments.
- Surprise your partner by doing something unexpected, such as giving him flowers, making her dinner, or introducing anal stimulation, as tonight is your first surprise night.

Insight for Her: Choose Fabrics to Make You Feel Sensuous

When you want to feel sensuous, choose fabrics that appeal to your tactile sense and heighten your awareness of your body. Men love silk, satin, cashmere, velvet, velour, leather, and fur because these fabrics feel soft and sensual to the touch. Silks and satins have a flowing feeling, and they drape the body without constricting it. Leathers and furs convey animal instincts. The feel of soft leather is akin to that of your skin. Brushing against a fur collar is reminiscent of stroking your hair.

If you're opposed to animal-based products, try synthetic furs, marabous, and latex leathers. Avoid itchy, scratchy, rough fabrics. But don't be afraid of metallic fabrics, sequins, and rhinestones. Things that add a little sparkle and glitter suggest opulence and festivity, and are a welcome addition so long as you don't overdo them.

CHAPTER 8

Rediscovering Each Other

Most people think of dating and courtship as something you do at the beginning of a relationship. In fact, the concept of "continual dating" can genuinely puzzle long-term partners, for they consider dating and marriage to be two distinct and incompatible concepts. Furthermore, many people view marriage or cohabitation as a total merger, even a stultifying stranglehold in which each person's unique needs are sacrificed and subjugated for the sake of the merger.

WHY YOU MUST COURT YOUR PARTNER

Nothing could be further from the truth. You can never fully know or truly own your partner. Just as you have to work hard every day to please your boss in order to keep your job, you need to seduce and please your partner on a regular basis if you want to stay together. No matter how stable your relationship is, it is never a full merger and no real assurances of everlasting love and devotion exist. Your daily efforts to make your partner feel special, sexy, and desired are the best way to create stability and enduring contentment in your partnership.

Just like you, your partner grows and changes, meets temptations, feels existential angst, and at times wonders what a new passion would feel like—which makes her secretly yearn to be seduced or long to sweep someone off his feet. No matter how long you have been together, you need to continually date and seduce your partner—otherwise, a stranger will become that surreptitious seducer who steals your partner away from your stagnated union.

Perception of total merger = rebellion, quest to seek freedom, and differentiation from your partner.

Perception of partial overlap = contentment, quest to retain connection and obtain greater merger with your partner.

So how do you go about dating and seducing your spouse? And how do you fit in another seemingly tedious task into your already over-burdened lives?

MAKE DATE NIGHT A PRIORITY

Each couple has its own degree of merger and differentiation needs. Try scheduling a date night at least once a month and preferably every week. In the ideal world, you should have at least one unencumbered evening per week to devote to your beloved—but the world is far from ideal. Do the best you can, but make sure you schedule your date far in advance and put it on your calendar, both to avoid last-minute conflicts and to build anticipation. You may also surprise your partner with a date by relieving him or her of responsibilities and whisking your partner away to the park—or to Paris!

When you're out on your date, make sure all of your attention is on your partner. Be fully present and totally mindful of your partner, and do not allow your eyes to wander—nothing will ruin your partner's mood quicker than your roving eye. Turn off your electronics—no texting allowed! You can simply hold hands and gaze at each other, or you can engage in lively discussions on interesting topics, such as news, philosophy, archeology, or world politics—anything unrelated to home, kids, and work.

You don't always have to have a traditional dinner date. Trying challenging, exciting activities together causes your brain to produce adrenaline, spiking your passion for each other. Plan and vary your dates—go to a concert one month, hit a bowling alley on another date, have a picnic together on a beautiful day, attend a museum or a sporting event, or venture to an amusement park.

SEDUCING YOUR PARTNER

If you're like most long-term couples, you abandoned the art of seduction a long time ago. Now you need to remember how to flirt with and seduce your partner. One of the easiest ways to flirt is with your eyes, engaging in a practice called the copulatory gaze. During this intense stare at the object of your interest, your pupils dilate, then your eyelids drop and you look away. This eye contact appears to trigger a primitive part of the human brain calling for either "approach" or "retreat" behavior. The copulatory gaze may be an evolutionary behavior embedded in our psyches, as other primates have been observed staring deeply into each other's eyes before engaging in coitus. If the person you're staring at is attracted to you, he or she is likely to smile or start a conversation. You can also use your eyes to wink or to look seductively at your partner.

When you're on a date, try to flirt with your partner as much as you can. Try various seduction signals to build the sexual tension between the two of you. Touch your partner's hand and arm as much as you can, or play footsie under the table. You can also try the "eyebrow-flash," which involves raising your eyebrows very briefly, for about one-sixth of a second. This suggestive move signals interest.

And, of course, a genuine smile is universally flirtatious. Couples smile at each other a lot more frequently in the courtship stage of a relationship than after the relationship is well established. As you get accustomed to each other, you look at each other and smile less and less often. Another way to seduce is by asking provocative personal questions, such as "What do you think is your sexiest feature?" You probably did these things without conscious intention at the start of your relationship, but now they require conscious effort.

CONSIDERING GENDER DIFFERENCES

You need to take gender differences into account. Daily seduction strategies, such as eye contact, compliments, and fleeting touches, are far more critical for women than men. Although men have sexual thoughts on average several times per hour, women think about sex on average about once a day. Women are also more likely to be distracted from sexual thoughts by pressing household and childcare responsibilities. Flirting with her, seducing her with your eyes, giving her fleeting affectionate touches, and making verbal innuendoes will remind her throughout the day of the intimate evening you are planning for her. Your attention keeps her mindful of love and erotically charged, preparing her for the night of passion.

Unlike male sexual desire, which is more robust and consistent, female libido constantly ebbs and flows like the tide of the ocean, subject to the hormonal fluctuations of her menstrual cycle. The impact of these hormonal changes on both her mind and body are quite significant. Most women feel substantially greater sexual desire at the midpoint of their cycles, when they are ovulating and most likely to get pregnant.

Additionally, women are subconsciously more likely to engage in extramarital affairs during their ovulation. One recent study of women playing an imaginary slot machine showed that different areas of the brain lit up in anticipation of a payout depending on the woman's menstrual cycle phase. So try to schedule date nights around the midpoint of her cycle, when she is likely to be ovulating—this is when she is most likely to be in a frisky mood.

Sex Rx Rule: *Seduction + Pursuit = Sex + Passion*

DAY 15

Today, use your eyes and smile to flirt with and seduce your partner. Practice a sexy gait and posture before your date, and when your partner is ready, give him or her a unique, sexy compliment. Then go out to a crowded place where others can lust after your partner—and they will, making you a tiny bit jealous and desirous for your partner all over again!

1. **Use your eyes to create romantic feelings.** Your eyes are your primary flirting tools. Intense eye contact, or "soul-gazing," transmits sexual energy, according to Tantric teaching. Engage your partner with your eyes by staring at him or her intensely for a few seconds, then dropping your eyelids and diverting your gaze— in other words, give your partner a copulatory look. The gaze will signal your connection and desire for your partner. Give your partner that look whenever you can—over breakfast or dinner, when you're bringing in groceries, or walking the kids to the school bus. Don't worry, nobody but you two will read the lust hidden in the look. And there is no harm even if your

kids catch you two flirting—studies show that children feel happier in households where parents freely display tokens of their desire for each other.

2. **Charm your partner with a genuine, seductive smile.** This is especially effective when you first see him or her at the end of the workday. A frequent complaint of long-term partners is, "I am tired of looking at her frowning/angry/distant face." Each genuine smile intended for your partner adds fuel to your Goodwill Tank. However, there is a big difference between genuine smiles and fake or managed smiles. When you smile spontaneously, your whole face, particularly your eyes, smile, but during a fake smile, only the sides of the mouth are used and none of the smile appears in or around the eyes.

   Research shows that the secret to creating a genuine smile is thinking positive thoughts or envisioning a pleasant scene or outcome. Imagine your favorite team or political candidate winning, getting a great bargain on amazing shoes, or, better yet, making passionate love to your partner. That pleasant mental vista should elicit a genuine smile, which will foreshadow the fun you'll have with your partner later on.

3. **Practice a sexy, seductive gait for your date night.** Your gait (walk) is an important nonverbal clue that your partner (and others) will consider when evaluating your sex appeal. Studies have shown that men and women are attracted to a more youthful gait, characterized by more shoulder sway, knee-bending, bounce, and loose-jointedness. Persons displaying such a gait are rated as sexier, happier, and stronger physically than those who walk with a less youthful gait. Women also prefer men who walk with a certain saunter, or

swagger in their step, whereas men prefer women who sway and swivel their hips.

If you want to adopt that sexy swagger as part of your seductive repertoire, rent some videos starring famous action heroes, such as Mel Gibson, Arnold Schwarzenegger, Russell Crowe, and James Bond star Daniel Craig, and try to emulate their swagger. A woman can learn to add sway in her hips by watching movies featuring seductresses such as Lauren Bacall, Jayne Mansfield, Marilyn Monroe, Sharon Stone, and Angelina Jolie. Put some bounce in your step, smoothness and looseness in your body movements, and you will be perceived as younger and sexier by your partner—and by others. Similarly, pay attention to your posture. Straighten your back and try not to hunch forward. Instead try arching your back when you're sitting or standing. Keep your shoulders back and your head high—it will not only make you appear taller but also more self-assured. If you have a natural tendency to stoop, remind yourself to arch your back and stick out your derrière.

4. **Give your partner a unique compliment.** When your partner gets all dressed up and ready for your date, give him or her a sexy but unique compliment. Stay away from banal compliments such as "You look great." Think about what makes your partner uniquely sexy and attractive and carefully choose a compliment based on that premise. Does she have adorable dimples, a cute smile when she giggles? Do you like the prominence of her hipbones or the curvature of her back? Do you like your partner's deep voice or debonair attitude? Or is it his ability to see the glass as half-full or her classy table manners that turn you on? Choosing unique words will show your partner that you know him or her better than

anyone else and that you truly appreciate and treasure your partner's unique sex appeal.

5. **Go out on a date.** Get dressed up and make an effort to project your sexiest appearance, which from now on you should always do on date night. Yes, it seems like a lot of work, but it's only once a week and your relationship is worth the effort. Put on your sexiest, sleekest outfit, do your hair, and put on your favorite scent. Women should try to wear high heels and makeup, if possible. You want to look different from the mundane everyday self your partner is accustomed to seeing. One of you should ask the other out. Although saying, "May I take you out to dinner?" to someone you live with sounds silly, it sets the mood for seductive role-play.

Now go out to a crowded place together. She should walk slightly in front of you, swaying and swiveling her hips, pretending you are not together. You should watch other men pay attention to your woman. Switch positions so that she can see how other women check out her man. Look at your partner through the eyes of these lustful strangers; imagine how they mentally undress your partner, ready to pounce on his or her flesh at any sign of sexual invite. Feel their lust for your partner and internalize it. You can kiss, hold, and fondle your partner on the way back from the date, but do not have intercourse. Save it for tomorrow after you seduce your partner all over again.

DAY 15 SUMMARY

- Use your eyes to create romantic feelings with a copulatory gaze.
- Flirt with your partner through genuine smiles.

- Practice a sexy gait and a confident posture for your date tonight.
- Give your partner a well-thought-out, unique compliment.
- Dress up and go out to a crowded place where you can watch others lust after your partner.

Bonus for Her: Don Sexy Legwear for Him

Many women abhor pantyhose—which is too bad, because most men absolutely adore them. Indeed, legwear worship is one of the most common male fetishes. Wearing fancy pantyhose is a great way to dress up a simple outfit and to feel sexy even when you forgot to shave or you desperately need a wax. To really wow him, put on a garter belt with vintage stockings—there's not a man who doesn't enjoy the pin-up look! It's a lot of trouble and not all that comfortable, but it's guaranteed to turn him on and set the mood for the evening.

Bonus for Her: Go Bare!

Whenever you dare, go bare for him. Go braless with a slightly see-through top, go pantyless under a long flowing skirt or tight capris, go topless on a topless beach. (Be reassured: Research has shown there's no correlation between going braless and breast droop.) Do it only on special occasions, such as when you're out on a date with your partner. The view of your erect nipples against the sheer fabric will tantalize him.

DAY 16

Today, continue to practice dating and seducing your partner. Give your partner token gifts symbolizing your desire. During courtship, couples frequently compete and show off to each other—practice this again with your partner. Couples also imitate each other more in the dating stage, so practice mirroring each other. Then go out and seduce each other!

1. **Give your partner a symbolic gift.** When couples date, they frequently give each other gifts, cards, and other small tokens of their affection, a practice quickly forgotten during marriage or cohabitation. You don't have to splurge here. Instead, think of how this small gift embodies your passion for your partner. The message of your gift should be, "I took the time to think of you because I care" rather than "I am giving you this gift in hopes of getting better sex." In other words, your act or gift should be a symbol of your love.

   Stay away from expensive, impersonal presents such as jewelry and gifts that are too cliché—instead of giving her red roses for her birthday, get her some pussy willows or wildflowers. If you have a talent for crafts, make something for your partner. Fill his glove compartment or her purse with her favorite candy. Unwrap some of the candies and sneak love notes inside. Buy a copy of the children's book *Guess How Much I Love You*, about a small rabbit and a big rabbit showing off how much they love each other (or buy any other children's book with a similar message). Then print out your pet names for each other and glue them over the names of the characters in the book. Or get a voice-message picture frame attachment. This recording unit will attach to the back of any picture frame you want and lets you record a ten-second message in your own voice. Your partner can play the message at any time. Surprise him by sticking it in his car or on one of his picture frames in the office.

2. **Get competitive with each other.** You can take up a sport or go gambling together, or find a topic you can debate enthusiastically. Playing competitive video games increases testosterone levels. Attending a book club or starting a blog about your favorite topic will make you more interesting to each other as you become involved in the world around you. Read the newspaper together or watch the news and ardently debate current topics. Intellectual sparring enlivens couples' interest in each other and resparks passion.

   Just make sure that your debates don't escalate into fights. Arguing elevates adrenaline (just as debating does). That's the reason why so many quarreling couples report great make-up sex—but it is not the sort of adrenaline rush we want you to use as an arousal tool. Although fighting can cause a temporary spike in your lust, every nasty argument is like a crack in the beautiful vase of your relationship, the one that holds the delicate flower of your passion.

3. **Mirror your partner's actions when you're out together.** Adopt a similar posture. This type of mirroring (even when done deliberately) increases your attractiveness in the eyes of the person you're mirroring. When flirting, you can use mirroring to create a feeling of harmony with each other, of presenting a united front to the world. If your partner crosses her hands in front of her chest, do the same; when he takes a sip of his drink, copy his move. If you can't duplicate a movement, approximate it; if she twirls her shoulder-length curls through her fingers, you can run your hand through your hair.

Do this mirroring subtly and casually—you will feel a sense of intangible connection to your partner, and your partner will feel the same to you.

4. **Try different flirting and seduction strategies.** See what seduction signals excite your partner—a copulatory gaze, touching your partner's hand, rubbing your lips seductively, or playing footsie under the table. Go dancing with your partner—after all, it's one of the oldest precopulation rituals. An old adage says that dancing is a vertical expression of a horizontal desire. Slow dancing is the perfect way to build your partner's desire, but if you know a club that mixes slow and fast songs, go there. Fast music has been shown to elevate heart rate and possibly increase your libido.

   If you can play a musical instrument and have a good voice, serenade your partner. As Shakespeare put it, "If music be the food of love, play on." If verbal seduction gets your partner all hot and bothered, ask him or her provocative questions such as, "What is one thing about your sexual past that you wouldn't reveal to anyone but me?" Of course, telling your woman that she turns you on and that you want to enjoy every part of her body before making love to her is the surest seduction strategy. Never assume that she already knows; a woman wants frequent reassurance that her partner wants her, not just any object with an orifice suitable for his sexual satisfaction. For many women, feeling sexually desirable is a way of feeling validated and valued.

5. **Get dressed up and make an effort to project your sexiest appearance.** Meet at a club or a bar, but drive there separately. Have your partner arrive at the club a little earlier than you and take a seat at the bar. When you walk in a few minutes later, go to the opposite

end of the bar. Pretend not to know each other. Your partner's job is to get your attention by flirting and approaching when you give the right signal and then to accomplish a successful pickup. You shouldn't acquiesce easily—instead, play a little hard to get. Eventually, accept your partner's cell phone number but don't give out yours. Call your partner a few minutes later and flirt on the phone, then agree to meet him or her by the car. Kiss and make out in the parking lot as if for the first time. When you eventually succumb to your partner's advances, pretend you're making love to your partner for the first time.

Remember, the male partner doesn't have to be the seducer this time. It's fun to reverse the roles, making the female partner the aggressive bad girl who unabashedly pursues the object of her desire. Switch the roles for your next date night.

DAY 16 SUMMARY

- Give your partner a token gift symbolizing your passion for him or her.
- Get competitive with each other by playing games and debating topics, which causes an adrenaline spike.
- Try different flirting and seduction strategies, both non-verbal and verbal ones.
- Mirror each other's actions when you're out together to present a united front to the world.
- Go out to a public place and pretend to pick up and seduce your partner.

CHAPTER 9

Revamping Your Sexual Script

Passion wanes in part when you and your partner become all too well-known and predictable to each other. It's not just the familiarity of your partner's body—it's also that you fall into the same boring, predictable sexual routines, such as always having sex missionary style in the dark on Saturday nights.

PREDICTABILITY PITFALLS

According to a *Women's Health* magazine survey, 68 percent of couples talk and touch after sex during their first year together. After five years, almost half are still into postcoital cuddling and conversation. But past the ten-year mark, only a third do anything other than nod off. Until the one-year anniversary, 25 percent try new positions a few times a month. That number drops to 15 percent after five years. After year ten, only 11 percent experiment at the same rate. This predictable sexual routine is known as a couple's "sexual script," which often becomes monotonous and boring.

By introducing novelty and sexual exploration, such as varying the place and time of your sexual activity (kitchen table during lunch?), trying new kissing techniques, discovering new "hot spots" or "moan zones" on your partner's body, and making up new sexual positions, you can often update your sexual script and respark the flames of your passion.

THE IMPORTANCE OF KISSING

Many people complain that their partners do not enjoy kissing. If you never liked kissing, try to figure out why and give kissing another chance. Although the act of kissing is not limited to the human species, humans appear to be especially programmed for kissing, with everted (protruding) lips uniquely adapted to give and receive oral pleasure. Kissing, both as foreplay and during intercourse, is a vital component of human intimacy. It connects the pleasure felt with an affirmation of affection, which amplifies the pleasurable sensations experienced during all other forms of sexual activity. The hormones produced during deep kissing send arousal cues throughout the body, sensitizing all of the erogenous zones.

In fact, kissing has such a tremendous implication of intimacy that, unlike sex, it usually cannot be bought—it is one act that most sex workers refuse to perform. A marriage is often sealed with a kiss, and many wedding ceremonies around the world include kissing rituals.

The pleasure potential of passionate kissing has been long recognized by humankind. Ancient Hindu books such as *Rig-Veda, Kama Sutra,* and *Ananga Ranga* viewed the kiss as the gateway to bliss, and in Tantric teachings a woman's upper lip was considered one of the most erogenous body parts due to a subtle nerve channel supposedly connecting her upper lip to her clitoris.

Kissing is not only intimate and erotic, it's also beneficial to your body—it relieves tension, akin to meditation, and helps reduce tooth decay by increasing production of saliva (which helps clean the mouth of harmful bacteria). Kissing may trigger physiological processes that boost your immunity—by sharing your bacterial flora, you are adding to your internal defense system and that of your partner. It may even help you lose weight—during a very passionate kiss, you might burn two calories a minute, which is double your normal metabolic rate. A deep tongue-tangling kiss also exercises all of the underlying muscles of the face, which some claim leads to a happier and even younger-looking countenance.

So do not rush kisses. Instead, savor them as you would your favorite drink or dessert. See if you can beat the world's record for the longest kiss—it took place on *The Ricki Lake Show* in 2002, where a couple kissed for a record thirty hours, fifty-nine minutes, and twenty-seven seconds!

Innovative Kissing Techniques

Kissing is an integral part of foreplay, and nothing will put her in the mood faster than kissing her slowly, passionately, and sensuously. Try these innovative ways to expand your kissing repertoire:

- **Brush Kiss.** As your faces come close, quickly brush your lips against your partner's as if to test the waters. This kiss is often used in conjunction with a hug.
- **Nibble Kiss.** While kissing your partner, ever so gently nibble on his or her lips. You must be very careful not to bite too hard or hurt your partner.
- **Tantric Frenulum Kiss.** Gently suck your partner's upper lip between your lips so that your lower lip lightly rubs his or her frenulum (that connective tissue inside the mouth between the upper lip and the gums).
- **French Kiss.** This kiss involves using the tongue to stimulate your partner's mouth and tongue while your lips are locked in a kiss. (The French call this "the English Kiss.") It's also known as the "soul kiss" because the passion expressed through this kiss is thought to be equivalent to exchanging portions of each other's souls. A shallow French kiss using your tongue to lick your

partner's lips and teeth is normally used to start a lengthy French-kissing session. From there a couple would move to deeper French kissing with their tongues stimulating each other's tongues and the roofs of each other's mouths. During deep French kissing, you can also very gently stroke your partner's tongue with your teeth.

- **Tongue Sucking.** During an open-mouth kiss, gently suck on your partner's tongue. The sucking pressure should be very light, but it can be gradually increased to draw your partner's tongue into your mouth.

- **Lip Sucking.** While your partner's lips are parted, gently suck on his or her top or bottom lip.

- **Tongue Flicking.** With your mouths close together, you and your partner both stick out your tongues and flick the tips of each other's tongues. The flicking can be either up and down or side to side. This is also known as the "porn star kiss" because it is mainly used in adult films and photographs to demonstrate that the participants are actually tonguing each other (and to avoid messing up the actors' makeup).

- **Ice Kiss.** This is one of the special-occasion kisses you can use to liven up your sex life. Put a small piece of ice in your mouth, then open your lips and kiss your partner, passing the ice with your tongue.

- **Food Kiss.** Take a small piece of fruit, soft vegetable, or candy and place it between your lips. Kiss your partner and either pass him or her a morsel or nibble one half of it while your partner nibbles on the other half. Fruits such as cherries, strawberries, and mangoes, and candies such as chocolate kisses, are particularly well suited for food kisses. Strawberries or cherries dipped in melted chocolate are delicious when shared in this fashion.

- **Flavor Kiss.** Take a small sip of your favorite drink. Leaving a little bit of it on your lips, kiss your partner and let him or her taste the flavor. Wines and liquors are particularly effective for leaving lingering flavors.

- **Menthol Kiss.** Apply lip balm with menthol or mint, such as Carmex, and gently rub your lips against your partner's to share the tingle. You can also use menthol to increase sensation in other oral interactions.

- **Trickle Kiss.** Take a sip of your favorite drink and trickle it slowly into your partner's mouth while kissing, using your tongue as a conduit to convey the liquid. Again, fruity wines and liquors make excellent vehicles for conveying your affection in a trickle kiss; champagne and other sparkling wines and juices add an extra fizz to the kiss.

- **Upside-Down Kiss.** When your partner is lying down, align your top lip with his or her bottom lip and kiss.

In all mouth-to-mouth kissing, start gently and work up to more passion in gradual stages. Anticipation adds to the excitement, and the more you take your time, the higher the excitement level can become. If you're worried about bad breath, be sure to brush your tongue as well as your teeth—especially if you have been drinking coffee or smoking—or chew on a lemon peel or mint, or pop a self-dissolving oral-care strip (made by Listerine) into your mouth before beginning.

BEYOND MOUTH-TO-MOUTH KISSING

After you've enjoyed mouth kissing, move on to kiss the rest of your partner's face. Don't forget the throat, sides of the neck, and tops of the shoulders. The area right behind the ears is especially sensitive, as is the back of the neck. Both of these areas can be reached easily when you are lying in the spoon position, and you are both on your side facing the same direction and cuddling together like nesting spoons.

MOAN ZONES TO EXPLORE

Alternate sides to allow each partner a turn at the other's erogenous areas. With each position shift, use lip kisses and hand caresses to maintain intimacy and arousal. Use soft, gentle kisses to start stimulating these areas, but if you feel your partner responding, increase the pressure of your tongue. You may even want to gently nip with your lips or teeth, especially on these back-of-neck and behind-ears zones.

MOAN ZONE #1: THE INNER-WRIST-TO-UNDERARM ZONE

Giving attention to this seemingly innocuous zone is a great way to start your foreplay. The inside of the arm is a very sensitive zone because the skin is thin there. Begin by taking your partner's hand and rubbing his or her fingers; then slowly proceed to the inner-wrist zone, gently brushing the tips of your fingers all the way up to the inner-elbow area, and then up to the underarm. If you are a male touching your female partner, the back of your hand can "accidentally" brush against her breast, but don't make it obvious.

MOAN ZONE #2: THE EYELID-TO-TEMPLE ZONE

The eyelid and the area above it has a great concentration of nerve endings, therefore giving your partner light kisses along the arch of the lid and onto the temple is a great way to start foreplay. The spot between the outer corner of the eye and the cheekbone is also very sensitive. After some nice passionate kisses, let your lips wander all over your partner's face, concentrating on these zones.

MOAN ZONE #3: THE CHEEK-TO-CHIN ZONE

The cheeks and chin are remarkably sensitive zones. Gently brush the back of your hand against your partner's cheek, touching or tracing his or her lips. Then stroke your partner's chin with your fingers, gently gripping it and drawing it to you for a soft kiss. A tip for a female partner: Men enjoy stimulation of the Adam's apple, such as kissing and nibbling from under the chin all the way to the chest.

MOAN ZONE #4: THE EAR-TO-NECK ZONE

Ears are one of the most forgotten of pleasure zones, yet many people are extremely sensitive behind and over their earlobes. Using kisses and a licking tongue or gently stroking finger, trace the folds of your partner's ears, nibble on his or her lobes, and gently stroke behind the ears and down the back of the neck.

MOAN ZONE #5: THE NECK-TO-SHOULDER ZONE

Believe it or not, this is the primary moan zone! Many men and a majority of women get totally turned on by stimulation of the area from the back and sides of their necks to the ends of their shoulder blades. Some women have even reported having orgasms from stimulation just in this area! Here, you can be a little less gentle: Hard kisses, even love bites, and firm massage of this moan zone will be appreciated. A tip for a male partner: Approach her unawares from behind, then plant rows of kisses from the back of her neck down her shoulders.

MOAN ZONE #6: THE NAVEL-TO-V ZONE

Some men and women enjoy their partner kissing and playfully touching their belly button, whereas others find it too ticklish. Twirl your tongue inside your partner's navel and observe his or her reaction. Some people enjoy stimulation of the V zone, that triangular area from the hipbones to the top of the genitals—it is more pronounced in people who are fit and they seem to enjoy having their partner direct attention to this area. A tip for a male partner: Many women fantasize about being held in a firm manly grip, so don't be afraid to put your hands on or around her waist. While holding her from behind and kissing the back of her neck, run your hands from her ribs to her pelvic bones, kneading and massaging the area in between.

MOAN ZONE #7: THE TREASURE TRAIL ZONE

This zone is more pronounced in women than men. It is the crease or line that extends across a woman's lower abdomen from one hipbone to the other, passing right over the top of the region covered with pubic hair (in its unshaved state). Make sure your kisses and fingers explore this trail before reaching her genitals. Many men also enjoy teasing stimulation of this imaginary line connecting their two hipbones.

MOAN ZONE #8: THE FEET ZONE

This is a conditional moan zone. Many men and women are self-conscious about their feet and might be reluctant to allow you to pay court to them. For others, however, it is a very erotic area. You can test your partner's attitude and try to remove any reluctance by bathing his or her feet, then drying them with a soft towel. Move from there to a thorough massage of the feet using edible massage oil; follow with oral stimulation. Start slowly, tracing the line of the massage strokes, and let your tongue travel between and around each toe before taking the foot in your mouth. If you hear moans, you have identified another prime target for arousing your partner.

MOAN ZONE #9: THE BEHIND-THE-KNEE ZONE

The skin behind the knees is thin and soft and very responsive to touch because the nerves are close to the surface. Some men and most women find that kissing and licking the crease directly behind the knee is very pleasurable—some even get shivery chills of excitement from such stimulation. From your partner's feet, work your way up to this zone and then focus on it, observing your partner's response.

MOAN ZONE #10: THE SACRAL CREASE ZONE

This zone is more pronounced in women, even though some men may enjoy it as well. It is the crease between the curve of the buttocks and the top of the thighs, known as the sacral crease. Stroking or running a finger along this crease usually produces a strong erotic response. A tip for a male partner: If your lover is on all fours or on her stomach and you are pleasuring her from behind, tease that area with a line of kisses or licks, bringing your lips closer and closer to her vaginal area with each pass.

MOAN ZONE #11: THE BUTTOCKS ZONE

The buttocks themselves are a strong erogenous zone for both men and women, but they need to be approached slowly, after the other moan zones have been stimulated. Light stroking or a teasing little squeeze while you are stimulating Zones 1 through 8 are fine, but save the hard stuff, such as firm squeezing or light spanking, until you have your partner well warmed up. A tip for a female partner: Grab your partner's buttocks tightly while planting a passionate kiss on his lips—he will love the boldness of this move.

MOAN ZONE #12: THE INNER-THIGH ZONE

This is the penultimate moan zone, the last area to be stimulated before moving to your partner's genitals. Don't overlook it though, as soft kisses and light fingertip stroking from your partner's knees right up to (but not including) the genitals will build sexual anticipation to the max. The teasing nature of such touches will be the spark that lights your partner's fire, as anticipation is the key to the ultimate arousal.

OUTERCOURSE, NOT INTERCOURSE

After you've experimented with new kissing techniques and explored new areas of your partner's body, don't jump into intercourse—try outercourse instead! Remember your high school days when you did all that dry-humping? Try this variation of dry-humping called femoral intercourse.

In this old-fashioned form of coitus, once used to preserve virginity or to prevent pregnancy in the days before birth control, the penis is inserted between the woman's thighs, either from the front or the back. The shaft of the penis can go between the labia to give pleasure to the woman, so long as the head of the penis lies outside. Femoral intercourse can produce some special sensations for the woman and is worth trying. With care, a man entering the thighs from behind can get the head of the penis to rub her clitoris and thus allow the woman to experience orgasm from femoral intercourse.

ARMPIT SEX

You can also try armpit sex, which offers a bit of variety, especially during a long bout of oral sex. By clasping her arms to her sides, a woman can create a moderately tight space in her armpits through which a man can thrust his erection. Penetration of the armpit can be made either from the rear or from the front, in either a lying or a kneeling position.

BREAST SEX

The female breasts can be the means of bringing a man to climax in breast sex, the so-called "boob job." This is normally done with the woman on her back, although it can be done with the woman seated and the man standing; or the man sitting and the woman kneeling; or the woman on top lying over the man (which is especially good for the women with small breasts). Cover the inner sides of your breasts with lube and let your partner insert his erect penis between them, either from the top (squatting or kneeling over the woman with her face near his butt) or from below (astride the woman's body). Hold your breasts together, forming a tight tunnel around the penis, and let him thrust back and forth to climax. In the "from below" position, you may be able to lick or suck the head of his thrusting penis as it emerges from between your breasts, adding to his pleasure.

FOOT PLAY

Before you engage in foot play, be sure your feet are clean and your toenails are trimmed and buffed to remove any sharp edges.

- Some men enjoy receiving "foot jobs"; that is, having their penises rubbed and stimulated to orgasm by a pair of female feet. It takes some dexterity to be able to maintain both feet in tight contact with the penis while moving them back and forth, and plenty of lube should be applied to the penis first to reduce friction.
- Another common sexual use of the feet is the "toe job," during which a man uses his big toe to stimulate a woman's nipples or clitoris or even inserts it into her vagina.
- Toe sucking is another favorite sexual sport.

ORAL SEX

Update your sexual script by performing oral sex on your partner in new ways. When you perform cunnilingus on her, try humming in addition to licking and sucking. With your lips firmly squeezing the clitoral sheath, and with perhaps a hint of suction to keep the seal between lips and clit tight, begin humming directly into the clitoris. Humming forces your lips to vibrate and act somewhat like a vibrator—the higher the pitch of your humming, the faster the vibration.

"Alphabetizing" is another way to change your oral sex routine. Use your tongue to trace each of the letters of the alphabet over her clit and vulva. Although there is nothing magical about the alphabet, the exercise ensures that your tongue is stimulating her from every angle and with the widest variety of strokes.

DEEP-THROATING

Master deep-throating to update your fellatio routine. Make sure you have sufficient lubrication—an erect penis will slide much easier along your tongue and into your throat if it is well lubricated. Once you're in position, slightly tilt your head back and extend the tip of your tongue just past your bottom lip. Flatten the back of your tongue just as you would if a doctor were using a tongue depressor to look in your throat.

Contrary to popular belief, do not try relaxing your throat muscles while performing deep throat; instead, force the back of your tongue down to create a larger opening for his penis to enter. Take a deep breath and slowly slide his penis into your mouth, moving it along your tongue. When you feel the urge to gag, pause and hold the penis there as long as possible, and then withdraw it, repeating this process as many times as you can.

With practice, you'll be able to take his penis in deeper and deeper until you can slide the entire length of it across your tongue and down your throat. When the head of his penis begins to enter your throat, try to use your tongue to over-come the extra resistance and to pull the penis in deeper. When you feel like gagging, pause for a moment, then extend your tongue out a little further; then pull your tongue back into your mouth, pulling the penis along with it, while swallowing.

Once you've mastered the art of deep-throating, you can also perform a so-called "throat massage" by making swallow-ing motions while his penis is in your throat. Your partner's pleasure can be intensified if you lick his testicles in the same time. You can also let your partner ejaculate with the entire length of his penis in your throat—this way, you will avoid the taste of the ejaculate because the head of his penis will be past the taste buds that are on the back of your tongue.

RISK TAKING

Although any sexual innovation in your script will add a sex-ual spark, engaging in thrilling, moving, sensation-seeking, or risk-taking activities will supersize your sexual passion for each other. When you engage in sensation seeking with your part-ner, or experience moving experiences together, your adrena-line surges, creating a mild anxiety in your body, a feeling of excitement and trepidation—akin to the way you felt when you first met each other. Thus, you effectively fool your brain into re-experiencing some of that initial infatuation for each other!

This boost in sexual interest triggered by anxiety and danger has been well documented in psychological research. One study demonstrated that people who meet on a shaky bridge find each other more attractive than those who meet on a steady one. In another study, those subjects who were told they would get a mild shock were more attracted to each other than those who did not.

Many anecdotal stories exist of people who suddenly fell in love when they survived a life-threatening event together (such as a bombing). Studies have shown that an adrenaline rush can also cause a desire to be close to someone, particularly your partner. No wonder pregnancy rates skyrocketed in New York City following the 9/11 tragedy.

Adrenaline-Boosting Activities

Mental Excitement
- Attending a moving concert
- Giving a public speech
- Watching a scary movie
- Going to a haunted house
- Reading an account of a catastrophe
- Visiting a cemetery
- Crashing a wedding
- Wearing something provocative

Physical Excitement
- Riding a roller coaster
- Horseback riding
- Rock climbing
- Experiencing heights
- Parasailing, skydiving, parachuting
- Fast driving or racing
- Zero-gravity experiences

INVENTIVE INTERCOURSE

You have an infinite variety of sex positions to explore and can find many great books devoted to them, beginning with the notorious *Kama Sutra*. Here are a few of our tried-and-true favorites to get you started—some of these are easy and others are challenging. Feel free to modify them any way you want, and to invent your own variations of these positions and their names for your Sexual Menu.

THE CAT MISSIONARY

The Coital Alignment Technique, or CAT, was first described in sexology literature in the early 1990s by sexologist Edward Eichel; however, a lot of experienced lovers have used it since the days of the *Kama Sutra*. This is sometimes described as "riding higher in the saddle," as it involves the man sliding his pelvis higher on the woman's body so that his pubic bone is brought into direct contact with her clitoris. To achieve this effect, the man must not only move his pelvis three to four inches higher on her body, but also he should not support himself on his hands or elbows. Instead, he should let the weight of his upper body rest fully on the woman. In addition, the man should shorten his strokes, rocking forward and back rather than fully withdrawing and thrusting. Each forward and backward movement should be only far enough to rub her clitoris with his pubic bone.

The obvious significance of this position is that it provides maximum clitoral stimulation for the woman and assists her in achieving orgasm. It also changes the angle of his penis to maximize friction on top of the penis and at the tip. Full insertion is likely to be difficult or impossible, due to the angle of the penis, but if the woman squeezes her thigh and pelvic muscles, she can increase the amount of friction to compensate. However, prolonged use of this position may not provide enough stimulation for the man to enable him to keep his erection; therefore, it may be necessary to switch to standard missionary from time to time.

THE LEG WORSHIPPER

This position requires a man to turn himself 180 degrees from the missionary, so that his head is between the woman's feet and her head is between his. The position bends the penis sharply downward and is uncomfortable for some men. This position benefits those who enjoy stimulation of their legs and feet, and it also gives the woman good access to her partner's buttocks.

THE COWGIRL

This position has the woman astride the man and facing him, as if seated on a horse, hence the name. Many varieties of the cowgirl are possible, depending on how she positions her legs. For example, she can squat (which allows higher and harder movement), kneel, or sit with her legs outstretched forward. In the latter position, she will usually lean back on her extended arms and let the man bounce her bottom. In the "reverse cowgirl," the woman faces away from the man and either squats, kneels, or sits on his "saddle" to ride his bone. A man enjoys this position because it gives him a great view of her bottom as she rides, which is stimulating to him as well. Also, from the reverse cowgirl, the woman can play with the man's testicles during her bouncing.

THE CROSS

In this position, the woman faces away from the man and lies flat across his legs, with her legs bracketing his head. Because of the way the man's penis is bent in this position, the primary motion is a forward-and-backward slide on his body, not an up-and-down motion. When the woman aligns her body so that her clitoris rubs against the top of the man's thigh, and her hands and breasts massage his feet, this position can be very stimulating; however, the limited range of motion makes it one to use sparingly during a sexual session.

UP AGAINST THE WALL

In this position, made famous in *Last Tango in Paris* and very popular in romance novels, the standing man places the woman's back against a wall or flat surface, with her legs around his waist, and thrusts into her at a slight upward angle. He will usually have to support her bottom with his hands to maintain the position. This position allows for very hard, deep thrusts, as her buttocks are rammed into the wall, yet it still offers substantial intimacy.

THE STALLION

In this classic position, the woman stands with legs apart, bending forward at the waist and resting her hands on a bed or other support. The man enters her from behind. This position allows for some very vigorous thrusts. It can be very good for G-spot stimulation if the man keeps his hips slightly higher than the woman's; the woman can buck backwards using her hands to push her behind into her mate's thrusts. It is also an easy position to assume when a long car ride raises your libido, as a car's hood provides the right height support for this position.

THE TRIPOD

This is a rather acrobatic position, and both partners must have approximately the same leg lengths. In this position, both of you are standing face-to-face. The woman lifts one leg high to rest on the man's shoulder or arm, allowing him to penetrate her. Because she is supporting herself, the position can be maintained longer than the wall and freestanding positions, but because she has all her weight on one foot, it does not allow for very forceful thrusting.

THE WHEELBARROW

In the wheelbarrow, another very acrobatic position, the woman stands on her hands with her legs supported by the standing man's shoulders while he holds her hips in position for thrusting at a 45-degree angle. This position doesn't allow for much room for thrusting, as the woman has to provide resistance with her hands on the floor. The reverse version of this position is a little easier. The woman's back is on the floor, with her weight mostly on her shoulders, and the man holds her hips up to his waist level. If she bends her legs backward over her head, he can penetrate her straight downward to create an unusual angle.

THE SIDESADDLE

In this position, both man and woman lie on their sides, facing each other. She puts one leg up and over his, allowing him to slide his penis in between her legs. This is an extremely relaxing position for both parties, and one that allows maximum intimacy—each of you has an arm free to caress your partner. Either or both of you can provide the back-and-forth work, and you can rest between more-active positions. Many couples use this as a transition phase between more intense and action-filled segments of their lovemaking, giving them a chance to cuddle and kiss while still joined together in intercourse. It is also an ideal position in which a man can practice longevity in "the saddle," as it puts minimal strain on him.

THE SPOON

This favorite position of many people places the man behind the woman, both lying on their sides. She bends her hips slightly to allow him to enter her from behind, like a pair of nested spoons. This position offers good intimacy, as the man can kiss the sensitive back of her neck and fondle her breasts with ease; however, the reverse is not true. She has to crane her neck backward to kiss or reach behind herself to caress, so this is a "man-giving" position. Variations on the spoon are also possible. For example, the woman can lift one leg to allow herself to be penetrated more deeply, and the man can lift his upper torso, supporting himself on his elbow for greater thrusting leverage.

THE SCISSORS

From either the sidesaddle or the spoon position, you can open up your joining until you are perpendicular to each other in the scissors position. Whether you are still facing each other or are both facing in the same direction, the sensations are just about the same. The scissors allows deeper penetration than either the sidesaddle or the spoon. It also affords more vigorous movement as well as more vaginal tightness and friction. To vary the scissors, the woman can bring both her legs together and bend at the hips while still on her side, and the man enters her from behind in a doggie-style scissors position.

CHURNING THE CREAM

This position requires a woman to lie on her back and pull her legs as far back as possible, knees up to her chest. Her partner then squats over her, penetrating her in this squatting position. It's a great way for him to combine sex and exercise!

SPLITTING A BAMBOO

Both man and woman are seated, facing each other. She lifts one leg, resting it on his shoulder, spreads her other leg out to the side, and leans back on her elbows. He moves forward, spearing her with his penis, and then leans back, supporting himself on his hands. Only limited movement is possible in this position, but the *Kama Sutra* claims that because both parties are staring upwards as they couple, this position leads to everlasting power and transcendence.

Sex Rx Rule: *New Action = New Attraction*

DAY 17

Today, begin revising your sexual script as you explore new ways of kissing. Find new hot spots on your partner's body. Make up your own Sexual Menu. Choose several new sexy songs to listen to together during lovemaking. Finally, make love tonight in a different setting—our favorite is a dirty little motel next door.

1. **Try a new way of kissing.** See the sidebar "Innovative Kissing Techniques" in this chapter for some ideas. Go for the longest uninterrupted kiss you have ever experienced with your partner or try a full-body kissing marathon.

2. **Find new hot spots or moan zones on your partner's body.** Venture beyond the genitals by viewing sex as a full-body experience. Try exploring every inch of your partner's body by looking for hidden hot spots or moan zones. See the sidebar "Moan Zones to Explore" in this chapter for suggestions of places to try. Don't be limited by the list. Think of your partner's body as a pleasure treasure map that you use to hunt for hidden arousal triggers. Some of the zones will be obvious—such as the neck—and others will take you by surprise. Who would have known some people get incredibly turned on from having their inner arms lightly brushed?

3. **Make up a Sexual Menu with your partner.** Include a choice of an appetizer, main course, and dessert, or make it an elaborate five-course meal, with soup, appetizer, salad, main course, and dessert. For example, appetizers could include the Tongue Flick and the Treasure Trail Zone. The main course should include intercourse with various sexual positions.

You can add weekly specials, allowing your partner to choose a sexy treat on your date night, his birthday, or your anniversary. Add real food to the mix, such as whipped cream on your nipples or melted chocolate on your genitals with a cherry on top, calling it a sundae or a banana split. You can include drinks with your menu such as a "body shot," allowing your partner to lick liquor off your chest. You can also have a take-out service and deliver the delicacies to your partner's office or a hotel room. Only you will know the full meaning of each item offered on the menu!

Sample Sexual Menu

Today's Chef's Special: Anal Delight

Starters
Sweet Eskimo Kiss
French Kissing with Deep Tongue Thrust
Tantric Upper Lip Nibble
The Sacral Crease with Whipped Cream
The Treasure Trail Kiss and Lick Mix

Main Courses
Flavored Fellatio
Cunnilingus a La Mode
Downward Dog

The CAT Over Easy
The Stallion Well Done
Split Bamboo

SIDE DISHES
Blindfold

Inversion

Neck Grip

Shoulder Hickey

Hair Pull

DESSERTS
Snuggles with Nuzzles

Postorgasmic Cuddle with Cherries on Top

Chocolate on Breasts Parfait

Selection of Ice Creams in Bed

4. **Choose several super sexy songs together. Here are a few favorites**:

> "Your Body Is a Wonderland" (John Mayer, 2002)
> "Crash into Me" (Dave Matthews Band, 1997)
> "Come to My Window" (Melissa Etheridge, 1993)
> "Push It" (Salt-n-Pepa, 1987)
> "Johnny and June" (Heidi Newfield, 2009)
> "Black Velvet" (Alannah Myles, 1989)
> "Crazy for You" (Madonna, 1985)
> "Melt with You" (Modern English, 1983)
> "Leather and Lace" (Stevie Nicks with Don Henley, 1981)
> "Time After Time" (Cyndi Lauper, 1984)

Create a playlist with your partner—it's fun to go sexy-song hunting together. Choose one that you always play right before making love—it will become a conditioned stimulus, and later playing that song will become an automatic trigger for your arousal.

Listening to music puts you in a sensuous mood and relaxes you. It also stimulates the parts of the brain that trigger happiness. And as you now know, happiness is a prerequisite for horniness.

To get more of a thrill from the music, turn it way up. Loud noise stimulates the *sacculus,* a small organ in your inner ear that regulates your balance and has a connection to the part of the brain responsible for hunger, sex, and hedonistic responses. That is why many people feel a pleasurable sensation when they listen to loud music.

5. **Modify your sexual routine tonight by changing the place and time of your sexual encounter.** Think of when and where you usually have sex. Now write down several scenarios containing an entirely different setting. Have you tried it on the kitchen table? Or bent over the piano? Straddling your partner on the toilet? What about outside for some alfresco sexual thrill, on the deck or a rooftop of an apartment? Decide which piece of furniture in the house you will inaugurate tonight (eventually you can do it on every one!) or meet for a quickie during lunchtime when the kids are in school—either at home, at the office, or at a local motel.

A cheap little motel will not break your budget and will do wonders for your sex life. Wear shades and pretend to look nervous and guilty, fidget in front of the counter as you insist on paying cash, and avoid direct eye contact with the clerk as you get the key—make him believe that you're having an affair. The thrill of doing something forbidden will electrify your desire for each other.

Of course, it may not be practical or appropriate for everyone—you have to rewrite your own unique sexual script, one that will thrill you and your partner. Whatever you do, when you make love today, it has to be in a different setting than usual.

DAY 17 SUMMARY

- Try a new way of kissing.
- Go pleasure treasure hunting on your partner's body to discover hidden hot spots or moan zones.
- Make up a Sexual Menu with your partner.
- Choose sexy songs together and turn them up loud to stimulate you and your partner.
- Modify your sexual script by changing the place and time of your sexual encounters, such as trying a "dirty little motel" experience.

DAY 18

Today, continue to modify your sexual script by exploring sexual acts you've never thought of before. You may not like all of them, but some of them may become part of your new sexual repertoire.

1. **Pursue a thrilling activity together.** Go for a bike or motorcycle ride together, explore an old cemetery in the twilight, hit a roller coaster, go bungee jumping or horseback riding, check out a haunted house or a historical murder scene, watch a psychological thriller or a disturbing movie about an apocalypse. Or come up with a few of your own ideas.

2. **Discover scents that stimulate sexual desire in you and your partner.** Some smells appear to have a strong positive effect on sexual arousal. The smells of chocolate and vanilla increase sexual stimulation in both men and women. Next time you want to put your partner in the mood, serve him or her a chocolate sundae or burn a vanilla candle. Try these other scents, too:

- Cucumbers and strawberries have been found to facilitate female arousal, whereas fish, freshly cut grass, and, quite surprisingly, roses have been found to inhibit female desire.
- Patchouli is also believed to awaken sexual energy.
- Musk closely resembles the scent of male pheromones, so invest in some cologne that lists musk as an ingredient.
- Peppermint energizes the body, sandalwood relieves tension, and jasmine is supposed to open the senses to new experiences.
- The smell of ylang-ylang is highly evocative of sex and is supposed to encourage verbal communication.
- The scents of cinnamon and gardenia are also considered to be aphrodisiacs.

Most of these scents are available as oils or incense sticks. Try one or two scents at a time and observe your partner's reaction. Keep your favorite ones handy to smell before engaging in lovemaking—the scent can actually make the experience much more memorable as olfactory memories are more lasting and vivid than visual ones.

3. **Try a new twist on an old oral sex routine.** When you perform cunnilingus on her, try humming in addition to licking and sucking. When performing fellatio

on him, go for deep-throating, mastering the gag reflex by swallowing when it happens. Use a menthol cough drop in your mouth when performing oral sex to produce coolness and a tingling sensation. You can put ice in your mouth to produce an even colder sensation or hot pepper sauce on your lips to add a burning sensation to the fire of the desire you're kindling in your partner.

4. **Try outercourse, or sexual acts that do not include vaginal or anal penetration. Some people can orgasm from nipple stimulation, others from closed-thighs sex, breast sex, or even armpit sex.** Many couples enjoy stimulating each other with their feet and even eyelashes and hair. Some men enjoy rubbing their penis around a woman's navel. Indeed, if the woman has sufficient fatty deposits around her waist, a man could actually engage in navel intercourse, similar to breast sex.

   The more different places on your partner's body you can use for stimulation and orgasm, the more sex will feel like a full-body experience, as opposed to genitally focused interaction.

5. **Find a new favorite sexual position tonight, or make one up.**

DAY 18 SUMMARY

- Pursue a thrilling activity together, such as riding a roller coaster or viewing a scary movie.
- Discover scents that stimulate sexual desire in you and your partner.
- Try a new twist on an old oral sex routine, such as humming, alphabetizing, or deep-throating.

- Try outercourse instead of intercourse, viewing sex as a full-body experience.
- Find or make up a new favorite sexual position after consulting sex manuals or websites.

Insight for Him and Her: Breast Stimulation

Stimulating female breasts is an almost universal turn-on for both sexes. Although it's less well known, many men enjoy having their nipples stimulated during foreplay and sex, too. Tantric teachings state that the woman's nipples correlate to her clitoris, and for many women, this is a truism. Some women feel there's a hotline between their nipples and their clit, so every action that stimulates their breasts has a double effect. Research shows that about 5 percent of women say they can achieve orgasm through nipple stimulation alone.

Although the erotic zone is less conspicuous in men, the male areolas have the same nerve connections to the pleasure centers of the brain that women have, so the techniques already discussed will work equally well when performed by a woman on a man. Some men even like to have their nipples pinched, bitten, or squeezed during intercourse or heavy foreplay.

Bonus for Her: Taste His Ejaculate

Many woman cringe at the thought of swallowing his ejaculate. Yet it is one of the most common male desires. Most women don't swallow because they don't like the taste of seminal fluid. However, if one swallows the fluid at the moment it is ejaculated, this taste can be avoided. You only taste the semen if you hold it in your mouth and let it come in contact with your taste buds.

If you can't manage to swallow, you should tell him that you prefer to watch him ejaculate, offering your body as a target, which will turn him on. The acts of pulling away or spitting it out can convey a feeling of rejection or revulsion, which is an emotional turn-off for most men. Although a man may get used to the idea that his partner doesn't swallow and may never ask, he will be ecstatic if you try to swallow or even just taste it.

Insight for Him: Mistaken Beliefs about Female Sex Drive

Some men are under the impression that women have no sex drive during their menstrual periods. In fact, the Hite Report found that 74 percent of women surveyed report an increase in desire just before or during menstruation. Ask her how she feels about making love during her period, and if she is willing, go for it. Remember, making love doesn't always have to mean intercourse—if you are not into making a mess, try the outercourse techniques suggested in this chapter.

PART 4

THE NAUGHTINESS FACTOR: DAYS 19–24

CHAPTER 10

Adding Playfulness to Sex

Reconnecting with the unabashed, expressive, unself-conscious, creative inner child within you can help you live more erotically. When you watch children play, you can see they are fully immersed in the activity. They're often so lost in their fantasy world that they're completely oblivious to what's going on around them. Children's play is usually unstructured, inventive, free of pressure, fluid and dynamic, flexible on rules, not goal-oriented, and done for the sole purpose of enjoying the game—it's a wonderful model for adult lovemaking. By turning off your orgasm-centered mind and treating sex as a fun game, you can liberate yourself from performance and response anxieties and allow for unscripted sexual enjoyment.

WHY FINDING YOUR INNER CHILD MATTERS

Unfortunately, most adults are totally disconnected from their childhood archetypes. They may even go so far as to repress or condemn the childlike qualities in themselves and others as immature, infantile, and incompatible with adult sexuality.

That's not the case. Acting silly, woozy, zany, wacky, goofy, and asinine to make each other smile and laugh as much as you can will often revitalize your relationship in unexpected ways.

How Laughter Works

Children laugh on average 300 times a day compared with adults, who laugh only about fifteen times a day. A good laugh relieves physical tension and mental stress, leaving your muscles relaxed for up to forty-five minutes afterwards. Laughter decreases the stress hormone cortisol, reduces inflammation, regulates hunger, and increases immune cells and infection-fighting antibodies, thus improving your resistance to disease. Laughter also relieves anxiety and depression as it releases the body's natural feel-good chemicals, endorphins, which increase your pain threshold and promote an overall sense of well-being. In addition, laughter improves the function of your blood vessels and increases blood flow, which can help protect you against a heart attack and other cardiovascular problems.

Most important, laughter improves your relationships by attracting your partner to you (and vice versa) and creating a greater bond. When people laugh together, they tend to make more eye contact, touch more, and report more positive feelings toward each other. Humor, particularly of a self-deprecating variety, is a great way to disarm defensiveness and diffuse an impending conflict. People who are perceived as funny are rated higher on their sex appeal by both genders. Women in particular find humor to be a turn-on and are more likely to bed men who make them laugh.

Playfulness can become a shortcut to arousal, in lieu of kissing, talking, or foreplay, particularly for women, who take longer to get turned on. Women and men differ when it comes to the pace of their sexual arousal. Male sexual arousal is spontaneous, whereas female sexual desire is receptive, or responsive to ambience, environment, and physical stimulation. Women take longer to get aroused than men, hence their need for longer foreplay.

To many men who view sex as a quick conduit to orgasm, foreplay is that ambiguous phrase that means additional work of an uncertain variety that stands in the way of instant sexual gratification. But foreplay doesn't have to always be massaging her body or kissing her back—it can simply mean "for play," or erotic games played before sex. Provocative sexual play and erotic games can spark her desire without putting pressure on him to engage in other forms of foreplay, and most men respond more positively to any behavior they consider sporty or gamelike.

PLAYING DRESS UP

A simple game to play together is good old dress up. Do you remember how much you liked to play dress up as a child? You weren't afraid to don various outfits, no matter how ridiculous you might have looked in them. Preschool boys can often be seen trying on girls' clothes and vice versa, with no embarrassment or shame—those feelings arise much later, triggered by the pressure of gender conditioning. Dressing up for sex is a wonderful way to keep your love life fresh and interesting, as the array of clothes and costumes you can wear is limited only by your imagination. Try on sexy lingerie, costumes, masks, corsets, spiked or high heels, leather gear, rubber and latex, ribbed and tickler condoms. Take advantage of post-Halloween sales to replenish your "naughty" closet.

Dressing up is exciting for the dresser, who anticipates the sexual enjoyment throughout the preparations. The surprise and novelty is also arousing your partner—the effort you took to get ready makes him or her feel appreciated.

PLAYING WITH YOUR FOOD

Many childhood games center around food, and eating and sex have been erotically linked in the human mind since time immemorial. The participants of orgies in Greek and Roman times often incorporated food as an integral part of their sexual play (colorfully portrayed in the movie *Caligula*). Vegetables, fruits, and other food items have been historically used for insertion and sexual satisfaction.

In the Mexican film *Like Water for Chocolate*, the heroine uses her cooking to sublimate her forbidden love and to transmigrate her passion into the body of her lover. In the equally riveting and renowned film *Chocolat*, the female protagonist uses her secret chocolate recipe to awaken desire and transform the atmosphere of a sleepy French town from sexually repressed to sexually obsessed. The acts of feeding and eating have also been eroticized in such films as *Tom Jones, Tampopo,* and *9½ Weeks*.

One way to play with your food is to use your partner's body as a food platter. You might have seen the *Sex and the City* movie in which Samantha Jones puts sushi on her naked body as she waits to surprise her lover on Valentine's Day.

Body as Food Platter

The practice of using your body as a food platter originated in Japan, where it is called *Nyotaimori*, or female body presentation (the male model version of this practice is *Nantaimori*). *Nyotaimori* is often referred to as "body sushi," because sushi and sashimi are usually served on the body of a naked woman, strategically covering her nipples and crotch area with food and flower décor.

Before becoming a living sushi platter, the person is usually trained to lie down for hours without moving.

She or he must also be able to withstand the prolonged exposure to the cold food. Before service, the individual is supposed to have taken a bath using a special fragrance-free soap and then finished off with a splash of cold water to cool the body down somewhat for the sushi. In some parts of the world, in order to comply with sanitation laws, a plastic layer is positioned between the sushi and the body of the woman or man.

PLAYING ON THE FURNITURE

You can add a variety of sex furniture to your boudoir collection to spice up your sex life:

- Wedges, or triangular-shaped pillows, are good for positioning a woman's body for the best G-spot stimulation.
- Love chairs and love swings are especially made to facilitate intercourse in the seated positions.
- Waterbeds, satin sheets, mirrored ceilings or floor-to-ceiling mirrored closet doors, and shower massagers also provide great stimuli for sexual arousal.

PLAYING WITH TOYS

Add playfulness to your sex life by experimenting with sexual aids. They're called sex *toys* because they're fun to play with. For example:

- Minimassagers (otherwise known as pocket rockets) are innocuous toys, used primarily for clitoral stimulation;

they're great for shy women who have never tried toys before.

- Vibrators (especially those with pulsation and a speed-control option) are handy to have by the bedside and can be used to provide extra stimulation to a woman's clitoris, during foreplay and during intercourse. A dual-action vibrator (otherwise known as a jack rabbit) provides simultaneous clitoral and vaginal stimulation. (You may have seen this one on *Sex and the City*.)

- Dildos can be used to provide vaginal penetration if the male partner reaches his orgasm too quickly or for double penetration during anal intercourse.

- Cock rings are used by some men to increase erection or prolong performance.

- Clitoral ticklers can be attached to cock rings to provide extra pleasure for the female partner.

- Ben Wa balls help arouse a woman in advance of sex play and can be used as a Kegeling aid.

- Feathers, fur gloves, ice, and many other objects can provide unusual sensations during foreplay and increase arousal for both partners.

- Anal beads (a string of balls on a cord) can be inserted in the anus during foreplay and then slowly withdrawn just before orgasm, bead by bead, adding anal stimulation to any form of sex play.

- Butt plugs, or conical-shaped dildos, are used for the same purpose as anal beads. They have a flared end to prevent the device from being lost inside the rectum.

- G-spot stimulators (such as Knobby-G by California Exotic Novelties) are curved in such a way as to reach that elusive G-spot.

- Vaginal barbells (like the Kegelcisor) are intended to exercise a woman's pelvic floor muscles, or Kegeling.

Kegel exercises, as we discussed earlier, enhance her orgasms, as well as prevent urinary incontinence.

- Clitoral pumps are applied to the clitoris, creating a sucking effect and increasing the blood flow to her genitals.
- Nipple clamps stimulate the nipples by applying varying degrees of pressure. The basic principle relies on the restriction of blood flood to the erect nipple. The best ones come with built-in vibration and can be used to stimulate other body parts as well.

You'll also find toys made for oral sex, including flavored panties and condoms, flavored lubricants, and massage oils. Play-acting and role-playing games offer fun ways to spice up your love life. Consider playing strip poker or other board, card, or video games with clothing removal as a "penalty" or sex games where the loser has to perform a sexual act on the winner.

Imaginative men and women needn't repeat the same lovemaking techniques week after week. The mind, remember, is the most important sex organ in the human body, capable of dreaming up an infinite variety of ways to make sex different and interesting.

Sex Rx Rule: Sex should be fun—so make it a game. Couples who play together stay together.

DAY 19

Today, add lighthearted, naughty playfulness to your sex life. Think of novelty as well as naughtiness, thus creating both conditions necessary for reawakening passion. Laughter and silliness will help you cope with stress and put you in a better mood—all the factors conducive to better sex.

1. **Laugh together.** Make each other laugh as much as you can. Text and e-mail each other jokes and funny stories, leave a funny message on your partner's voice-mail, or play a practical joke. Find some dirty jokes and sexually suggestive jokes or images on the Internet and share them with your partner. Invite your partner to a comedy club or a roast or try laughter yoga. When your partner walks in the door, act silly—as silly as you possibly can.

   Research shows that people who enjoy silliness are more likely to be happy by a factor of one-third. And don't be afraid to do it when your partner had a stressful day. Your playfulness will help dissipate your partner's stressful mood because emotions are contagious. If you make the effort to be lighthearted and silly, you'll infect your partner with good cheer—the type of emotional contagion we should all try to spread.

2. **Court like a child.** Before you knew that attraction could terminate in sexual intercourse and orgasm, you sublimated your urges through physical games and athletic contact. Remember how you courted a kid you liked back in kindergarten? You probably teased and chased her, pushed him against the wall, or pinched, shoved, and tickled her.

   In the same way, call each other silly (but not insulting) names, chase each other around the bedroom, play naked tag and hide-and-go-seek, have a pillow fight, wrestle in bed, pull her ponytail, give him a wedgie, pin her down, throw clothes at him, play "doctor" and "show me yours and I'll show you mine." Marvel at your partner's genitalia as if you were seeing it for the first time.

   Use baby language to describe your genitalia, such as weenie, wee-wee, and bum-bum. Look up funny names and slang for genitals such as the Gristle Missile, One-Eyed Wonder Weasel, Thrill Drill, Blue-Veined Junket Pumper, or Trouser Trout for the penis and Meow Mix, Shaven Haven, Silk Meadow, Pussy Willow, Fish Gills, Meat Curtains, and Vertical Beef Sandwich for the vulva. Have a good laugh and make up your own unique silly nicknames for your nipples and genitals.

3. **Tickle each other.** Tickling is another erotic sport often noted in childhood sexual play. Some people find it arousing to be tickled on the torso, under the arms, and down the sides of the ribs, as well as near the belly button. Experiment with a light tickling touch, such as running a fingertip across your partner's ribs, to see whether it produces a positive response. Some people are not ticklish on their torso but have very ticklish legs or feet. If so, you may want to add tickling to your foreplay repertoire.

   A more erotic form of tickling is called *pattes d'araignee,* or literally translated from French, "spider's legs." Use the tips of your fingers to apply the lightest possible touch, aiming to touch not your partner's skin but the tiny hairs on sensitive areas such as the chest, belly, insides of arms and thighs, armpits, and the back (not on the genitals, though). The extreme lightness of the touch is electric and erotic, like a light breeze brushing over the skin. You can use various props, such as feathers and furs, to further experiment with your partner's sensitivity. Tickling can also be part of an erotic game. One partner can tickle the other—if you laugh, you have to give the tickler an erotic kiss in a place of his or her choosing.

4. **Eroticize your meals.** To add playfulness to your sex life, buy vegetables and fruits that resemble sexual

organs or that have acquired erotic significance, such as bananas and mangoes, and slowly, passionately consume them in front of your lover, deliberately stimulating them with your lips and tongue as you would his or her sexual organ. It is especially effective when done, unabashedly, in public or in front of a stuffy ceremonious waiter in a formal restaurant. The subtle suggestion of sexual desire in a public place triggers a release of adrenaline as it combines suggestiveness with the exciting fear that others will understand the "private" signals being transmitted.

Even during private sex play, you can call attention to your favorite erogenous zones (such as the belly button) with his or her favorite fruit (such as cut-up star fruit or grapes) and tell your lover that his or her dessert is ready. Use your tongue to tease the pimento out of an olive; insert a banana to test your gag reflex; and eat peaches to perfect the art of cunnilingus. Or smear your body with fruit and whipped cream and tell your partner to lick it off. Do exactly what your parents forbade you to do—play with your food in the naughtiest way imaginable!

5. **Pick a role to play tonight.** What sort of naughty scenario would appeal to both of you? Have her dress up as a naughty schoolgirl in need of some corporal discipline from you, her stern headmaster? Drape her in queenly finery while you play the suave courtier seeking her favor? Have her pretend to be a belly-dancing concubine in your harem? Play nurse and patient, or doctor and patient, and explore each other's bodies with stethoscope and fingers?

Get a costume and/or some props, such as a fake stethoscope (you can pick up one in most dollar stores) and create a little scenario. You don't have to be a talented thespian to enjoy acting in your personal screenplay. And if you are really adventuresome, cross-dress and let her play the male role while you act out the female part—you will both learn a lot about each other by observing how you see one another.

DAY 19 SUMMARY

- Laugh together.
- Reconnect with your inner child by acting infantile and playing childhood games—naked!
- Tickle each other, looking for your partner's favorite spots.
- Eroticize your meals by playing with your food.
- Play a role, such as nurse-doctor or warden-prisoner, and act it out tonight before making love.

DAY 20

Today, continue to reconnect with your carefree, creative, mischievous inner child. Make out like teenagers. Decide which sexual games you'd like to play. Get messy while taking a bath together. Turn your partner into a food-serving tray. Choose a new role-play game tonight.

1. **Pretend you're horny teenagers.** Wear something adolescent such as hip-hugging torn jeans, sweats, cap backwards, sneakers, a school uniform skirt, or knee-high socks. Text each other silly abbreviated messages, such as "U R 2 COOL." Sneak around all day stealing kisses and coping a feel. Share a beer together. In the evening, go for a drive together, park the car somewhere private,

turn on some rap or pop music, then make out in the car and dry hump each other. Suck on each other's neck until you create hickeys. You can terminate your teenage experience with some oral sex in the car, but do not have penetrative sex—save it for your role-play tonight.

2. **Choose which sexual games you want to play** (and add them to the Jar of Our Desires). Make up a private trivia game—the winner gets to choose an act of sexual pleasuring from his or her partner. If you like card games, try strip poker. If you're not into intellectual games, choose a more physical game to re-enact together. You can stage a treasure hunt with clues leading into the bedroom where your partner will discover the ultimate prize—you naked on the bed!

   Many couples have fun with pretend animal play—having fun while releasing their animal instincts. She can pretend to be taming her partner, a wild and undomesticated horse. Horseback riding is a sexual turn-on for many women. The reasons are obvious: The feel of a big muscular animal between her legs, bouncing up and down on her vulva and buttocks, is sexually stimulating. A woman may use the man as a "pony," riding on his back, using a crop on his buttocks, and generally making him carry her around as if she were at a rodeo. Some women are able to achieve orgasm by riding on their partner's back, especially if they are riding bareback. You can also pretend that she is a pussycat and he is a dog chasing, climbing, and biting her, or that he is an elephant and she is a snake seductively slithering up his leg and wrapping herself around his trunk. For other sexual game ideas, watch Roman Polanski's movie *Bitter Moon*, which is replete with sexual acting out and role-play.

3. **Engage in water play when taking a bath or shower together.** Do you remember how much you enjoyed

water games as a child? Recreate that feeling of mis-chievous abandon with your partner as you splash and sprinkle water on each other. Don't worry about spilling it on the floor—be as messy and as wild as you want. Work up lots of bubbles in a bubble bath and blow them on each other—strategically cover your body parts with bubbles and check each other out in the mirror, giggling. Use the showerhead as a massager to stimulate your partner all over his body, including the genitals.

Play with rubber duckies and other toys, squirting them at each other. Pour some water on your partner's head, then wash her hair. Rub shower gel all over your partner's body—just make sure to avoid the genital area, where it may burn. You can alternate between being silly and sensuous, playful and probing. You may get turned on and even have an orgasm, but do not make it your goal. Simply play with the water and your partner's body, allowing the game to take its own course. After the bath, pat each other dry with warm towels and rub moisturizer on each other.

4. **Turn your partner into a food-serving tray.** Because you have just taken a bath or a shower, now would be a good time to serve as your partner's food dish. Make sure to wash any traces of soap or shower gel, towel dry yourself thoroughly, and do not use heavy moisturizer—if you skin tends to be dry, put on natural oil such as almond or olive oil. Spread a sheet or towel on a bench, couch, or floor, and then lie down naked. Let your part-ner spread any food he or she desires on your body, from snacks such as crackers to fruits and vegetables, cut up into flat discs so that they don't roll off. You can pick up sushi to get close to the true Japanese practice. Just avoid placing sugary substances on your partner's genitals, as

these can promote yeast infections, or spicy things that may cause irritation.

5. **Pick another role-play for tonight, but this time add more props and toys.** Remember when you were a child, you found alternate uses for common household objects, such as brushing your hair with a fork? You can use common household objects such as scarves and belts to blindfold, tie, tease, or spank your partner. Spoons can provide some temperature-related play if you cool the metal ones in the refrigerator or warm the plastic ones in the microwave. Cucumbers can be used for penetration (wash them first).

If your budget and time allow, browse an adult store alone or together. Choose a sexy costume, such as that of a French maid, and some props, such as a duster, and pick up some sex toys as well. If you are a toy novice, purchase a small vibrator for her to stimulate her clitoris, such as a pocket rocket. She can tantalize her clitoris while you are doing her doggie style, which will provide both of you with some delightful stimuli.

If she enjoys vaginal penetration, choose the classic jack rabbit for her. A great toy for him is a vibrating penis ring, which can be angled to provide extra clitoral pleasure for her or stretched over a testicle to stimulate his perineum. Of course, one of you may feel really adventurous; in that case you can get his-and-hers anal beads or plugs.

DAY 20 SUMMARY

- Act like horny teenagers to tap into memories of your carefree adolescent desire.
- Choose which sexual games you want to play, from strip chess to animal imitation.

- Engage in silly water play when taking a bath together.
- Turn your partner into a food-serving tray as you feed yourself right off his or her body.
- Pick another role-play for tonight, this time using more props, either household objects or toys obtained from an adult store.

Insight for Him: Turn Up the Heat

Being warm is critical for female arousal and orgasm. One empirical study found that some women couldn't reach orgasm if their feet were cold. So turn up the heat, lie down with her in front of a blazing fire—or get her some cute socks. When her body temperature is elevated, her nerve endings are more receptive and sensitive. But don't overdo the heat. If she gets too hot, she'll be burning up instead of getting turned on—no woman likes to feel like she is in the sauna while making love.

Bonus for Him: Find Her G-spot

To locate the "G"—the elusive spot that stimulates a female—face your partner while she's lying on her back. Insert your index or middle finger into her vagina as far as it will easily go. Then crook it upwards (toward yourself) in a come-hither motion, sliding your fingertip along the front wall of her vagina, until you find an area that is rougher than the rest of the vaginal wall. (Make sure your fingernails are clipped short and buffed with an emery board or nail file before you do this—sharp fingernails will definitely spoil the effect!) This roughish and ridged area, usually about an inch or two inside the vaginal canal, is the G-spot, and touching it will often cause a woman to react with surprise or pleasure.

If you don't get a reaction, don't be too shy to ask her if she feels especially sensitive when you touch what you think is the spot. You may need to use a fair amount of pressure to find the spot because it's located deep inside the vaginal wall. Sometimes it helps to use your other hand on the outside of the pubic mound to lightly massage the area your crooked finger is touching to intensify the effect.

This spot is more sensitive and larger during arousal. But if she thinks too hard about your finding it, she may lose her sensitivity. If you don't find it right away, drop the effort and try again later when she is more aroused and not expecting it. Because not all women are G-spot sensitive, don't get discouraged if you can't get a special reaction. Your finger stimulating her vagina may be pleasurable to her anyway. You can always use a special curved G-spot toy that usually works when manual methods fail.

CHAPTER 11

Using Erotica to Enhance Arousal

The term "erotica" refers to works of art (including literature, photography, film, sculpture, and painting) that depict erotic stimulation or sexual acts, or that are intended to incite sexual arousal.

Visual images are critical to arousal. When you see someone attractive—symmetrical, healthy, and vigorous-looking, feminine or virile—the visual areas of your brain are activated. And those areas make up more than half of your brain! The male brain is particularly responsive to visually arousing material. Researchers from Emory University found that, even though both sexes reported interest when watching sexual material, a part of the brain that controls emotions and motivation called the amygdala is much more activated in men than in women. No wonder the majority of men get so easily turned on by visual pornography—the male brain is evolutionarily programmed to get excited by sexually provocative imagery.

Refer to the Appendix for a list of books and films you may enjoy reading and watching in order to enhance your arousal.

FINDING EROTICA THAT APPEALS TO WOMEN

When it comes to sexual arousal, women are less visual than men, but they still appreciate and get turned on by an erotic sight. More and more women admit to enjoying visual erotica—from material as mild as Calvin Klein ads to as wild as porn videos. Research shows that even women who do not believe they're aroused in response to visual erotica often experience physiological arousal (quantified through vaginal photoplethysmography, which measures blood flow in the vagina).

Although women may experience physiological arousal watching pornography, male-oriented pornography is often distasteful to women because it portrays artificially enhanced women as objects designed solely for male sexual satisfaction. Many women admit to feeling jealous when their partners stare at women who are thinner, bustier, younger, always sexually excited, and willing to perform any sexual act enthusiastically.

CHOOSE TOGETHER

Discuss her concerns and choose visual erotica together. She may feel self-conscious about her postbaby appearance, or she may feel inadequate compared to the actress's deep-throating skills. If she has any discomfort, seek female-oriented erotica, such as that produced by Candida Royalle. These films appeal to female fantasy by featuring realistic storylines, romantic settings, and prolonged foreplay. Most men report enjoying Royalle's films along with their female partners (although a few may suppress their yawns during the extended kissing scenes). In addition to Royalle's films, which are specifically geared toward women, you'll find plenty of tasteful, artistic male-oriented choices that she will love, such as the slow, sensuous work of Andrew Blake or the fast-paced music video "art core" of Michael Ninn.

START WITH ART

One of our favorites is *Zazel: The Scent of Love,* an award-winning, highly acclaimed adult film produced by the Dutch erotic photographer Philip Mond. The film is premised on an elusive search for a scent for a love perfume. It consists of a dozen themed sequences that include powerful iconography drawn from mythology, religion, literature, film, and even Jungian psychology. Elaborately designed and shot imagery includes sirens, mermaids, angels, demons, and women's genitalia portrayed as beautiful orchids.

Even more conservative and sexually inhibited women have found the movie incredibly arousing, despite the fact that it features explicit and fetishistic acts. An almost universally positive female response to *Zazel* suggests that it is not the explicitness of the acts that women find objectionable and obscene but the crude, vulgar, and prurient way they're often portrayed. Women can appreciate the most explicit sexual act when it has a highly artistic value.

NONVISUAL EROTICA

Whereas men tend to get sexually aroused almost exclusively in response to visual stimuli, most women are more likely to respond to sounds and smells. Women are also very responsive to verbal erotica, both aural and written—hence the popularity of romance novels. This may be partly due to the fact that the brain areas responsible for processing sounds and smells are more closely linked with areas interpreting sexual arousal in women. Women get turned on by sensuous words, erotic stories, and romantic plots. No wonder it's said that men fall in love with their eyes, women with their ears. The best seducers in history, such as Casanova, Rasputin, and Don Juan de Marco, had a way with words. Of course, men are also responsive to sexual talk—hence the popularity of phone sex.

THE PHEROMONE FACTOR

Women are also more responsive to pheromones, the biochemicals emitted by the human body that serve as sex attractants. A woman is more likely than a man to be aroused by her partner's smell, particularly when she's ovulating. In the words of Jennifer Aniston, "There is no sexier smell than that of the man you love."

Smell plays a tremendous part in human attraction for both men and women. Neurological evidence indicates a direct connection between the olfactory bulb at the top of the nose and the septal nucleus of the brain, the erection center. When you get sexually aroused, the erectile tissue in your nose swells up. No wonder a large portion of people who have smell disorders develop sexual dysfunction.

A number of scents stimulate desire, including lavender, licorice, and cinnamon. But no scent is as arousing as the natural scent of your partner, especially fresh genital sweat. We call it "olfactory erotica," and we encourage you to use it to turn on your partner. Try mimicking Napoleon Bonaparte, who sent an urgent missive to his beloved Josephine: "Home in three days. Don't wash."

APPEALING TO ALL SENSES

When you're trying to turn on your partner, include as many senses as possible. Put on your favorite cologne or swipe your finger under your armpit or your genitals and let your partner smell you. Whisper what you plan to do to your partner and verbalize your arousal. Draw your partner's attention to the visual elements of your desire: your erect nipples, your wetness, your engorged genitals. In the throes of passion, you are a work of erotic art for your partner, so don't be afraid to boldly display your eroticism!

> **Sex Rx Rule:** *Men have eyegasms; women have eargasms and nosegasms.*

DAY 21

Today, begin to use verbal and visual erotica to increase your sexual arousal. To some extent, you experienced the power of aural erotica when you recounted your peak sexual experiences and did the fantasy-driven guided masturbation. Today, further attune your senses to erotic expression by reading, seeking out, watching, and sharing erotica that appeals to all your senses.

1. **Choose a book of erotic stories or poems.** Go to the bookstore and browse the erotic fiction section or order a book online. You'll find a list of suggested erotic short-story anthologies in the Appendix. You can also download erotic stories and listen on your computer, iPod, or iPad from *www.penthouseletters.com*, *www.playgirlmagazine.com*, or *www.ravenousromance.com*.

   You can do this exercise alone and surprise your partner. Most women like romance novels, so pick a sizzling one for her and highlight your favorite paragraph. Men usually prefer visual stimuli—the type of illustrated stories published by the *Penthouse Forum* will get him all hot and bothered. By reading erotica, you'll learn the poetic language of lust.

2. **Share erotic imagery with your partner.** Find sexy images online, print them out, or e-mail them to your partner. They can be pictures of other men, women, couples, body parts, or even objects, because objects

can be erotic as well—a sleek racecar, a sexy bed, a photo of a Tahitian hut in a perfect tropical paradise—any image that engenders erotic longing.

Eroticism is all around, and now it's time for you to begin actively seeking it out and sharing it with your partner. Together, rate the images according to their degree of eroticism, then stash away your favorites in your secret drawer in the bedroom for your and your partner's eyes only! You can even start a collection of erotic art or sculpture—voluptuous fertility goddesses and sex gods with unnaturally large and erect penises. If you travel, attend erotic art exhibits and museums of sex—many cities have one, including New York and Barcelona.

3. **Leave explicit sexual messages for your partner.** You can do it on voicemail or by e-mail. You can also write explicit instructions of what you want your partner to do to you and post your description in your bedroom. Or leave the explicit instructions where your partner will find them and think about them throughout the day. Take a photo of one of your body parts and text it to your partner. Include a naughty line to go along with it. "Sexting" between you and your loved one can get you both ready for a romp!

4. **Rent, buy, or download a sexy movie.** It can be a classic Hollywood film such as *9½ Weeks* or a European classic such as *Belle du Jour* or *Last Tango in Paris*—so long as it's R-rated or NC-17 material. One study showed that when couples watched a romantic video together while holding hands and discussing the experience, their levels of oxytocin, a chemical involved in bonding, rose dramatically, particularly in women. Another study found that men enjoy romantic films much more than the macho stereotype suggests. In the

Appendix, you'll find a list of favorite romantic films that have an intense erotic edge.

If you're familiar with the movie you're watching, you can even fast-forward to your favorite sex scenes. You don't have to pay close attention to the movie—instead, discuss it. Talk about the arousal you're experiencing; share with each other how the sex scenes make you feel, foreshadowing what will happened next. Pretend you're the protagonists and invent what you would do if you were enacting this movie. Feel free to discuss what it would be like to have sex with the protagonists—your partner imagining you with the movie villain or heroine is a good type of jealousy that can respark passion.

5. **Make love to each other while talking dirty.** Begin by leaning over and whispering sweet nothings in each other's ears. Use terms of endearment as well as the cute nicknames you came up with for your private parts a few days ago. Then get more explicit in your language. Forget about clinical description of sexual parts and acts. Express admiration for his swollen cock; talk about her creamy tits with pert nipples and juicy, dripping pussy. Lust has its own language; don't be afraid to speak in "lustese" to your loved one. Look up words for genitalia and sexual acts in different languages and share them with each other. Saying *"baise-moi"* in French will make both of you feel particularly naughty.

DAY 21 SUMMARY

- Choose a book of erotic stories or poems and read them together.
- Collect your favorite erotic images and share erotic imagery with your partner.

- Leave explicit messages on your partner's voicemail and engage in "sexting."
- Get a romantic film with an erotic edge and watch it together.
- Make love to each other while engaging in explicit sex talk.

DAY 22

Today, continue to delve into the world of erotica, making it more explicit and vivid than before by reading, watching, and making your own porn. Don't be afraid; it's for your eyes only! Incorporate "olfactory erotica" into your life (a keepsake scented with your partner's sexual secretions). Scents are powerful, memorable aphrodisiacs.

1. **Write an erotic story, poem, or song for your partner.** It doesn't have to be a great literary work of art. It can be inconsistent and even silly at times, so long as it aims to arouse your partner. Keep it focused on your romance and make sure it culminates in a passionate lovemaking experience between the two of you. Incorporate some of the fantasy elements your partner shared with you a few days ago, but leave out the fetishistic elements for now.

   Make your partner the sexy, desirable protagonist in the story and yourself the protagonist's object of desire. Remember that men prefer more explicit descriptions of acts and body parts, whereas women prefer romantic descriptions of plot, ambiance, feelings, and desirability. Try to guess what would really turn your partner on and incorporate it into your plot.

Use erotic stories found on the Internet (such as *Penthouse Letters*) as a guide.

2. **Give your partner a scented keepsake.** During the medieval times, lovers often exchanged locks of hair or kerchiefs as expressions of undying love and affection. Give one of your intimate garments, such as a bra, undershirt, underwear, or panties, as a erotic keepsake. Most women choose their lovers' sweaty undershirts, whereas most men prefer the lacy panties their lovers have worn. Put your keepsake in a Ziploc bag to preserve your scent, and present it to your lover.

   Or you can create your "personal perfume sampler." Soak a piece of paper in your sweat or genital secretions and slip it in your partner's wallet. Ask your partner to do the same for you. Use the sampler to take in your partner's aroma when he or she isn't around and fantasize about being with your partner.

   If the thought of giving each other scented keepsakes makes you a little squeamish, remember that sweat and genital secretions contain pheromones that trigger arousal. In fact, most men are subconsciously drawn to ovulating women because their genital secretions contain special pheromones that increase their attractiveness to men. So if you plan to save a pair of your panties for him, don't wash the ones you wore during your midcycle.

3. **Rent, buy, or download an adult movie.** Discuss what you want to see beforehand and make sure you're both comfortable with what you're going to watch. Does she have bi-curious fantasies and want to check out lesbian erotica? Does he prefer mature women and want to watch something that includes sexually aggressive "cougars"? Does she want lots of kissing and fore-

play? Will that bore him? Use the notes you took in your His and Her Pleasure Manual during your fantasy exploration a few days ago to figure out what both of you would enjoy watching.

If at any time one of you finds the film not stimulating or objectionable, stop watching and choose something else. You can compromise a bit if your fantasies diverge, but you don't have to force yourself to watch something you dislike or find offensive for the sake of your partner. The idea is to select movies that turn both of you on, will expand your sexual horizons, and encourage you to experiment and explore previously unknown sexual terrain.

4. **Make your own visual erotica.** Play the photographer/model game in which one of you poses for the other in an erotic photo shoot. If you're feeling brave and uninhibited, you can actually photograph or videotape each other using a camera, video camera, or webcam. If you're not comfortable with any permanent evidence of your naughtiness, you can shred or erase the images afterwards or simply pretend that you're taking them.

The idea is to create visually exciting images for each other's mind, regardless of whether the actual images are immortalized or destroyed immediately after your game ends. Shamelessly displaying your body, flaunting your sexuality, and making love to the camera, while your partner gives you orders to undress and open yourself up, is uniquely erotic.

5. **Make love to each other like porn stars tonight.** Porn-star sex differs a great deal from the real deal. Porn stars have sex under the bright lights and in front of other people. Female porn actresses usually start out wearing sexy outfits and then quickly disrobe,

frequently leaving some token clothes on, such as a cor-set or thigh-high stockings, and they always leave their high heels on. Porn stars frequently change positions, and they seem to do so seamlessly, while remaining connected in penetrative sex. They talk dirty to their lovers, and they are incredibly vocal in their moans and groans. Male porn stars almost never ejaculate inside a female porn star—instead they proudly shoot their ejaculate on a woman's breasts, buttocks, or face.

Pretend you and your partner are porn stars. Act shamelessly brazen in front of the imagined camera, be vocal about your pleasure, and express insatiable desire for sex and for each other. When he comes, make a big deal about it: Display it to the imaginary viewers, smear it all over your body, and taste it. After you are done, discuss the fantasized experience with each other. Did it make you feel objectified, used, or desired?

DAY 22 SUMMARY

- Write an erotic story, poem, or song about your partner, using the fantasy elements you learned a few days ago.
- Give your partner a scented keepsake, such as a pair of panties you've worn.
- Watch an adult movie you've chosen together after dis-cussing triggers for your arousal.
- Make your own visual erotica by taking real or pretend explicit photos and videos of each other—either for keeps or to be destroyed after the game is over.
- Make love like porn stars tonight by keeping the lights on and being vocal.

Insight for Him: Her Sharp Sense of Smell

A woman's sense of smell is keener than a man's. However, her sensitivity does change during the course of her menstrual cycle. Estrogen increases her smell acuity during the first half of her cycle, when she's most fertile and most sexually responsive. Don't go overboard on cologne and deodorant, as your woman is probably aroused by the natural smell of your body, particularly when she's ovulating.

Insight for Her: Keep Your Bodily Insecurities to Yourself

Don't ask him whether he sees that cellulite on the back of your legs. Men tend to see the general picture, which is a lot more than the mere sum of your body parts. But if you continually criticize your body and invite him to join you on a flaw-finding mission, he'll have no choice but to start noticing those imperfections. If you keep on showing him your cellulite, he'll eventually believe it's there, whether he sees it or not.

Instead, draw attention to the parts of your body you like. Wear a long necklace to emphasize your cleavage, a belly-button piercing if you like your stomach. If your thigh cellulite still bothers you, wear sexy thigh-highs and he'll never complain.

CHAPTER 12

Expanding Sexual Horizons

Expand your sexual horizons to include practices that lie outside plain-vanilla sexual interaction. Some people consider acts such as anal sex to be perverse, but there's nothing perverse about them. They're performed by many normal, well-adjusted couples all over the world. So open your mind and take a walk on the wild side.

ALTERNATIVE SEXUAL PRACTICES

Of course, taking a walk on the wild side means something different for every couple, depending on their experience, degree of sexual sophistication, and prior experimentation together. Is deep-throating or tasting your partner's ejaculate something you would like to learn? Is anal sex something your partner has expressed interest in and that you're curious to try? Have you fantasized about being watched or watching others perform sexual acts? Or about being tied up and dominated? Are you interested in trying out threesomes, swinging, or multiple sexual partners?

ANAL SEX

One of the most common taboo sexual acts is anal sex. The anus is highly sensitive to touch and richly endowed with nerve endings, and it contracts rhythmically during orgasm. For these reasons, the insertion of a finger, tongue, sex toy, or penis into the anus and rectum can be quite pleasurable. The famous *Kama Sutra* considers anal sex a key to releasing certain sexual and physical energies, not something taboo or forbidden. Indeed, the landmark sexual study by Kinsey et al., in which the researchers did a series of interviews between the years 1938 and 1963, concluded that the anal region has erotic significance for about half the population and that 47 percent of men and 61 percent of women had tried anal sex. They just didn't talk about it back then.

In 1972, the famous butter scene from the controversial Bernardo Bertolucci film *Last Tango in Paris,* brought the idea of anal sex to the average moviegoer, and many more people have tried it since. Some women say they are able to have bigger and more satisfying orgasms from anal sex than they can from vaginal sex. Even those who do not feel comfortable going all the way with anal sex find it pleasurable to include anal foreplay in their sexual pursuits.

Women enjoy anal stimulation because of the close proximity of anal and vaginal nerve endings. Most men also enjoy some anal stimulation because of the anus's proximity to the prostate gland, which plays an important role in male orgasm. The prostate produces most of a man's ejaculate (except for the sperm, which is produced in the testicles). It is located inside the man's body, in the region between the anus and the base of the scrotum, and is accessible primarily through the anus. When you are facing each other, insert a finger up to about the second knuckle into his anus, then curl your finger slightly upwards toward yourself in a "come hither" motion—this will usually stimulate the prostate gland.

When a man ejaculates, the entire area around the prostate, including the anus, throbs quite noticeably. Stimulating this area even lightly during orgasm causes some men to have orgasmic spasms and some to experience much-longer periods of orgasm with greater intensity and volume. Because of this, some men enjoy a butt plug, a cone-shaped plug that can be inserted into a man's anus during sex and left in position until orgasm. Anal stimulation of the prostate is known as "prostate milking" and has been shown to be beneficial in prostate health and preventing prostate cancer.

EXHIBITIONISM AND VOYEURISM

Many people associate exhibitionism with sleazy, perverted flashers who get off by opening their trench coats and exposing their genitals in public places to children and adults. They think of voyeurism as something dirty old men do, spending their quarters at peep-show booths or gawking at attractive passersby. But exhibitionism and voyeurism between consenting adults in appropriate circumstances can enhance your sex life.

A glimpse of a purposefully flaunted sexual organ can be extremely arousing to the onlooker. The lure of exhibitionism was powerfully demonstrated by the infamous Sharon Stone–flashing scene in the movie *Basic Instinct*. Use the power of exhibitionism by dressing seductively or wearing no underwear on your next adult outing. Petting in the movie theater, doing a quickie in the car parked in a dark parking lot, or posing for your lover's camera are all examples of mild exhibitionism that can spice up an otherwise stale sex life. If you travel a great deal and own a laptop, invest in a webcam so that you can excite your partner by masturbating on the cam.

Before engaging in exhibitionism or voyeurism, ascertain that the venue is not accessible to children and that your behavior would not be considered illegal or offensive to other adults.

BDSM PLAY (BONDAGE, DISCIPLINE, SADISM, AND MASOCHISM)

BDSM is gaining wider acceptance among the general population. When most people think of BDSM, they think of a cruel, brutal sadist whipping or beating a pitiful, helpless masochist. These types do exist, but most people who practice BDSM do it very differently. It involves one partner in a loving relationship (the submissive) surrendering control of her or his body and independence to the other partner (the dominant) for the purpose of increasing their mutual sexual pleasure. The submissive's voluntary surrender of will is key, because that is what defines BDSM as a sexual mind game. Without that, no one should engage in BDSM.

Contrary to popular belief, the submissive, not the dominant, person is really in control of a BDSM session, because the submissive's pleasure defines the action and makes it possible. The dominant has the responsibility of justifying that submission by creating the pleasure for both parties. Some people experience better sexual enjoyment through BDSM because they need permission to feel pleasure or because this is the only way they are able to surrender control—by passing the responsibility for their pleasure to their partners.

Special Preconditions for BDSM Play

Before engaging in BDSM, you and your partner need to establish some ground rules regarding trust, discussing your mutual desires, and creating and obeying the safe word.

ESTABLISHING TRUST

You need to trust each other so that the submissive partner knows that no matter how the game is played, in the end, the dominant partner will try to give the pleasure the submissive seeks, and that afterwards, the dominant will "undo" the submissive's surrender, restoring both of you to your normal positions in your relationship. *That trust must be established first.* For that reason, lovers should have had some experience in bed together and should have built trust through previous interactions. Alcohol or drugs should not be used in a BDSM scene, as the dominant needs a clear head and good judgment at all times, and the submissive needs to know when pain thresholds have been reached.

DISCUSSING YOUR DESIRES

Before you get started, discuss what you want, including your limits—*particularly the submissive's limits*—in advance. You must have a reasonably good understanding of what might be pleasurable and what will not be. Intimate talk about secret fantasies each of you has had or role-playing games (like the "naughty schoolgirl" being spanked for some infraction or the "bad driver" being arrested and searched by a sexy but stern police officer) are ways in which lovers can learn each other's desires and limits.

UNDERSTANDING AND OBEYING THE SAFE WORD

The submissive should always have a "safe word" that he or she can use to stop the BDSM play at any time if it becomes too intense or painful. The safe word or phrase should be something simple and easy to remember, but not normally used in BDSM play. "Red light" is a common safe word; you can even agree on "yellow light" to be used if the submissive is getting scared that the play might devolve into a red-light situation.

Orgasm Denial Games

In orgasm denial games, the dominant causes the submissive to be erotically stimulated close to the point of orgasm, but then denies its completion, perhaps repeatedly, over the course of hours, or even days. The purpose is to raise the submissive's sexual tension to the boiling point so that her orgasm, when finally permitted, is especially powerful and satisfying.

You can do this in hundreds of different ways, from binding the submissive to the bed and teasing him with feathers, furs, light oral or finger play, spanking and flogging, to simply ordering him to submit to sexual practices or masturbation over and over without allowing him to climax. The submissive is brought to the point of approaching orgasm but stopped just short of it, until she cannot bear the tension any longer and the release is permitted.

Enforced Availability Games

In another BDSM game, the dominant orders the submissive to be ready to have sex at a particular time, or continuously for hours or days at a time. A male dominant may direct what his female submissive should wear, how she should prepare herself, and what she must do when he is ready for her. A female dominant might require her male submissive to keep his penis semierect or to wear a cock ring underneath his clothing. Making her insert Ben Wa balls into her vagina will keep her mind on sex while she's at work or while the dominant is away, or she might be required to masturbate at regular intervals to keep herself continually wet, ready for penetration at any moment the dominant chooses for sex. He might be required to go shopping for toys, such as dog collars or whips, that the dominant may want to use on him—just the act of shopping for such things will give him sexy thoughts. All of these should be things that make you think continuously about the sex to come, as they will increase the arousal level for both of you beyond its normal state.

Role-Playing Games

Role-playing is one of the most frequently used and fun ways of engaging in BDSM play. For example, if you are into spanking or bondage, you can role-play all the traditional disciplinary scenes: teacher and naughty pupil; guardian and naughty ward; prison warden and prisoner; storekeeper and beautiful thief; or boss and mistake-prone employee. The number and variety of different scenarios is limitless. Having a selection of props and even costumes makes the play even more exciting.

The preparations for a scene should be incorporated into the play, as setting up props and getting into costume make the participants think about what's going to happen, thus increasing the sexual tension for both of you. You can also draw up a list of "punishments" for everyday mistakes; every time the submissive makes one of these mistakes, an opportunity for a BDSM scene arises. Indeed, for some couples with a standing punishment list, a BDSM role-play opportunity is always available, with the submissive initiating the action by "confessing" to a supposed fault or by the dominant "accusing" the submissive of a particular mistake. When the other party "accepts" the confession or "admits" the mistake, the game is on. In such games, punishments might be determined by dice or games of chance, increasing the tension of the scene.

Lovers of bondage games, during which the submissive is "tortured" by being stimulated but not permitted to orgasm (until the dominant decides to allow it), can also use role-playing as a part of the BDSM sessions. Many varieties exist, including the captured spy, the Spanish Inquisition, the pirate and his noblewoman victim, the conqueror and the queen, the hijacker and his hostage, and the crooked policeman who will agree to let the criminal off if she allows him to have his way with her. For many couples, role-playing not only enhances sexual arousal, it's fun for its own sake.

Sexual arousal can also be increased by having the submissive "perform" in public or semipublic situations. Just the fact that she might be discovered by strangers increases her excitement and thus her sexual tension. For example, you might require the submissive to wear a butterfly vibrator while you hold the remote control when you go out to a party, to a restaurant, or to the movies. Or you might require her to go without panties and to provide you with various views during a sporting event, in a theater, or while sitting in a bar. How about ordering the submissive to go into a public restroom and masturbate and then bring you her wet panties to prove that she did it?

Sensory Deprivation

Many BDSM games involve sensory deprivation. This works on the premise that depriving a person of one of his senses increases the keenness of the others. For example, blindfolds are often used on the submissive to prevent him from seeing what is coming next, as surprise is adrenaline-producing and stimulating. You might drop candle wax on your blindfolded and bound partner, which is especially exciting because he cannot see where the drops will fall next. (Be sure to test the heat of the wax on your hand first to make sure it isn't too hot, and remember that the greater the height from which the wax falls, the cooler it gets. Never drop wax on the face or directly on the genitals—though the areas around them are fair game.)

Similarly, earplugs can deprive the submissive of hearing, and a gag can prevent her from talking or protesting what is happening to her. However, if you are going to use gags, make sure your submissive has a way of signaling a nonverbal safe word to stop the action if it gets too intense.

EXPLORING OTHER PLEASURES

Besides the practices we've discussed in this chapter, you may want to venture out and explore other fetishes, such as golden showers. Or, share your sexual enjoyment with other partners in a ménage à trois or through swinging. Whatever you and your partner decide to try, don't allow outdated ideas of what is "proper" (as far as sex is concerned) to inhibit your sexual expression. Don't let someone else's prescription of right and wrong dictate what's right or wrong for you and your partner or hinder your sexual creativity. If you're both mentally healthy adults who want to please and be pleased (rather than hurt or injure), and if it feels good for both you and your partner, then it's an act worth trying.

> *Sex Rx Rule:* Explore outside your comfort zone for erotic renewal. Nothing is "abnormal" between two consenting adults.

DAY 23

Today, expand your sexual horizons by agreeing on a new sexual repertoire for you and your partner.

1. **Agree on the wild side you wish to explore and then buy some fetish items to go along with your idea.** Would you like to try swallowing semen, anal sex, or double penetration? Experiment with fetishistic gear?

Tie each other up? Do you think it might be fun to have sex in a place where you can possibly get caught? Would you like to try ménage à trois or attend a swingers' club and just watch?

Shop for props to go along with your fantasy. It can be a paddle, a pair of fuzzy handcuffs, nipple clamps, or an invitation to the next swingers' party. You can shop online, bid on eBay, or check out a local adult store.

2. **Write a short erotic story about your partner.** This time go outside your and your partner's comfort zone and make it a kinky story. Keep your partner as the main protagonist of the story and yourself as the protagonist's love interest, but you can include additional characters to spice things up. Decide whether you and your partner will be the dominant or submissive characters. You can both be required to submit as you're captured by knife-wielding pirates and turned into their slaves. Or choose from elements of anal sex, exhibitionism and voyeurism, bondage and discipline, or multiple partners. Again, feel free to browse online stories and use those stories as guides.

3. **Play the enforced-availability game.** Decide who will be the dominant partner today. The dominant one will order the submissive to be ready to have sex at a particular time, directing what the submissive should wear, how she should prepare herself, and what she must do to get ready. All of these should be things that make the submissive think continuously about the sex to come, as they will increase his or her arousal level beyond its normal state.

4. **Spank your partner.** Put your submissive across your knees or in front of you in the kneeling position. Play with his bottom, squeezing and testing its firmness and

fullness while telling your partner what you are going to do to his bottom, and how it will look in a few minutes.

First, spank your submissive over his clothing, then order your partner to remove it and spank his bare buttocks. Alternate a dozen or so spanks with rubbing your partner's bottom, using firm but very sexual stroking to spread the warmth all over. Cupping your palm slightly with fingers together is the best way to spank, as it makes a good smacking sound and reddens the skin without causing excessive pain. A slow tempo, with an irregular rhythm, is the best technique, as the moments of anticipation between each stroke add to the tension. Play with your partner's genitals in between spanks, but not enough to bring on an orgasm.

5. **Make kinky love to your partner tonight.** Order your partner to stand in front of you naked as you slowly and deliberately examine her body. Slowly and sensuously shave your partner before getting in bed. Put a blindfold or earplugs on your partner so that sensory deprivation can enhance his other senses. Try inversion—have your partner's head hang down from the bed while you're making love. The blood rush enhances orgasms for many people. Pretend to overpower him or her—many men and women enjoy a sense of being overpowered during lovemaking.

DAY 23 SUMMARY

- Agree on the wild side you wish to explore and buy some fetishistic items to go along with your idea.
- Write a kinky short erotic story about your partner and share it with him or her.

- Spank your partner by putting him or her across your knee and using your hand.
- Have kinky sex with your partner tonight by incorporating elements of sensory deprivation and inversion.

DAY 24

Today, continue to push your erotic boundaries by making everything kinkier—your spanking and your lovemaking. Switch the dominant-submissive roles today unless one of you has a strong preference or aversion toward one of the roles.

1. **Watch an erotic mainstream or porn video that includes themes you would like to explore tonight.** If you want to try anal stimulation, watch the famous butter scene from *Last Tango in Paris*. If you want to learn the psychology of dominance and submission, watch *Story of O*. Or watch the infamous Sharon Stone–flashing scene in the movie *Basic Instinct* to get your submissive partner ready to engage in exhibitionistic acts.

2. **Spank your partner, but this time do it in the context of "traditional" disciplinary role-play, such as teacher and naughty pupil or prison warden and prisoner.** Use implements to spank such as a belt, a wooden spoon, a brush, a paddle, or a cane. If you use an implement, start with light strokes. The first dozen or so strokes with an implement are the most painful, as your partner's buttocks will eventually become slightly numb from repeated stinging and his body will release endorphins, the natural painkillers. Work into harder strokes gradually so that he or she experiences more pleasure than pain.

3. **Make the submissive partner perform an act of exhibitionism.** Go out into a public setting and require him or her to wear a vibrator or a vibrating penis ring while you hold the remote control. Order the submissive to go into a public restroom and masturbate, and then bring wet underwear as proof of self-pleasuring. Punish him if you don't find the underwear to be wet enough. Now require the submissive to go without panties and to provide you with various views of her naked genitalia upon demand.

4. **Make even kinkier love to your partner tonight.** Blindfold and tie your partner up in some way. Begin by kissing your partner's neck, then give him love bites (hickeys). If your partner is particularly responsive to the stimulation of his neck and shoulders, you can even try harder stimulation by sinking your teeth into the shoulder muscle while gently grabbing and pulling his hair. For many women, neckbiting is erotically charged because it invokes the Dracula prototype of the dangerously predatory male sexualized in many vampire novels.

   You can engage in some temperature play by touching your partner with an ice chip and/or dripping some hot wax on her. Tease her with various props such as feathers and ticklers; bring your partner almost to orgasm, but deny its release until she screams for mercy.

DAY 24 SUMMARY

- Watch an erotic mainstream or porn video that includes themes you would like to explore.
- Spank your partner by putting him or her across your knee and using an implement such as a belt.

- Make your submissive partner perform acts of exhibitionism by requiring him or her to go without underwear.
- Have even kinkier sex with your partner tonight by incorporating elements of sensory deprivation, bondage, temperature play, and orgasm denial.

PART 5

THE LOFTINESS FACTOR: DAYS 25–30

CHAPTER 13

Delaying Gratification

Anticipating an exciting event is often a greater pleasure than the event itself, a phenomenon called "rosy prospection." Positive anticipation of the enjoyable experience often magnifies its pleasure when it finally arrives. In one study, subjects were given gift certificates to an upscale restaurant. Those who had to wait a few weeks to go there for dinner reported greater enjoyment of the food than those who were able to dine sooner. Psychologists have even come up with a fancy term for how anticipating an enjoyable experience magnifies our pleasure—they call it "the pregoal attainment effect."

THE JOY OF ANTICIPATION

Unfortunately, most people don't fully relish the joy of anticipation, choosing instant over delayed gratification whenever possible. Instead of enjoying the process, we focus on the goal.

You've probably experienced this yourself, when you've fallen prey to the "arrival fallacy," the belief that you'll be happy when you finally get something you want or when you arrive at a certain destination. But as Friedrich Nietzsche put it, "The end of the melody is not its goal."

Getting too much of a good thing too easily, even something as great for you as sex, will lessen your enjoyment of it.

Psychologists call this phenomenon "the hedonic treadmill." You get accustomed to what you have all the time, until you no longer derive much pleasure from it.

How can you have your cake and eat it, too? By occasionally depriving yourself of the things you have all the time and by purposefully creating a sense of frustration, you can experience a longing for what you've grown accustomed to.

Temporary deprivation gives you a different perspective, distanced and loftier. That distance allows you to gain a new level of longing and desire. How often do you devour food without really relishing its taste? It's only when you diet that food takes on a different, deeper meaning—the fantastic flavor of the forbidden fruit.

Couples who are separated by business travel on a regular basis involuntarily create such deliberate deprivation. These couples often feel greater passion and desire for each other than those who are always together. Kahlil Gibran put it so well when he said, "Let there be spaces in your togetherness."

CREATING DELIBERATE DEPRIVATION WITH PRESCRIPTIVE PROHIBITION

One way to create deliberate deprivation is through "prescriptive prohibition," or scheduling off-sex days, followed by all-sex days. Many religions have such prescribed periods of sexual abstinence. These enforced religious abstinence rituals have been reported to create intense desire and longing in those who practice them. We humans want the very things we cannot have—we are tempted to overstep boundaries, violate prohibitions, and break taboos to get them. It is through the creation of the forbidden that we spark temptation and create desire.

Psychoanalytical psychologists believe that sexual prohibition is deeply interconnected with temptation in our archetypal collective unconsciousness—we have all heard about Eve's inability to resist sexual temptation despite the threat of losing Paradise. Biological psychologists believe that violating prohibitions is tempting because the fear of penalty produces anxiety, which spikes the adrenaline our brains often mistake for sexual desire. And then there is the obvious—the harder it is for us to get something, the greater thrill we feel when we do finally acquire it. So create occasional obstacles and prohibitions to free access to each other's physical being in order to increase longings and lust for each other.

THE PHENOMENON OF REACTANCE IN CREATING DESIRE

In addition, being told we cannot have something or do something creates a feeling termed "reactance" by psychologists. Reactance is a psychic rebellion against the feeling that your freedom of action is being encroached upon. When you think someone is threatening your ability to make personal choices, you tend to shift in a direction exactly opposite to that being urged upon you—an effect of reactance. It is a powerful psychological phenomena demonstrated in many studies. For instance, researchers noted that when the legal drinking age was raised from eighteen to twenty-one years of age, the alcohol consumption of those aged eighteen to twenty-one significantly increased! After examining all the variables, the researchers concluded that reactance was the reason. When young people felt their freedom to drink alcohol was abridged, they responded with rebellion.

Some therapists use the principle of reactance when they practice paradoxical intention with couples who have lost their sexual spark. When paradoxical intention is used, the patient is told to do the opposite of what the therapist wants him or her to do. By instructing the couple not to have sex for a prescribed period of time, the therapist hopes to create that feeling of reactance, which leads to righteous indignation and the temptation to violate the prohibition and restore the couple's freedom to do whatever they want.

We have successfully used such paradoxical intervention with our clients. One couple came to therapy because they had not had sex in more than a year. The wife, Natalie, complained that her husband, Bob, stopped initiating all sexual advances. At first, she attempted to initiate sex, but after a while she felt hurt and rejected. When they came to us, neither one of them was willing to initiate the first sexual move.

After their first session, we instructed, "For the next month, you are not to have any sexual contact with each other whatsoever. Natalie, you cannot kiss or touch Bob. Bob, you cannot touch Natalie in any sexual manner until we instruct you otherwise." Both of them looked at us in disbelief. Then Bob retorted with righteous indignation, "What do you mean I cannot have sex with my wife? That's what being married is all about. Nobody can tell me I can't touch my own wife."

We then explained to him that such a conditional prescription is our prerogative to use as a therapeutic intervention. Moreover, if either of them violated our rule, they had to pay us a "rule violation penalty" of $500. They left the session baffled and discontent. We were supposed to fix their sex life, not eliminate it altogether! But, as we predicted, Bob was only able to last two days before he barged into their master bedroom in the middle of the night and made passionate love to Natalie. They both said it was "some of the best sex we've had in years." We did not charge the couple a rule violation penalty. Instead, we explained that our demand was a way to intensify their psychological reactance to our prohibition as part of our paradoxical intention intervention.

THE PHENOMENON OF THOUGHT SUPPRESSION IN CREATING DESIRE

Another psychological phenomenon you can use to bolster your desire for your partner is called "thought suppression." The gist of the thought suppression theory is that when we actively attempt not to think about something, we end up thinking about it all the time. In the original study of thought suppression, the subjects who were asked not to think of a white bear ended up being totally preoccupied with the thought of the animal not only during the experiment but for a while after.

Trying to suppress exciting thoughts intensifies the excitement. We often use this paradoxical trick to get our clients to think more about a specific topic. Asking someone not to think about sex produces a strong preoccupation with it—sex being as exciting a topic as it gets! When you practice this exercise, you will see how having sex with your partner will quickly turn into "a white bear."

USING DELIBERATE DEPRIVATION

To tap into the temptation power of taboos, you can schedule off-sex days or weeks, followed by all-sex days or weeks, and watch your frustration and desire grow as you excitedly anticipate the day when you can again make love to your spouse. Not being able to have access to your partner during those days will augment and intensify your desire for each other. The prohibition against sexual activity during the off-sex days must be firm and definitive and include all sexual contact.

You must take your prohibition seriously during the off-sex days by agreeing upon a rule violation penalty if one of you violates such prohibition by succumbing to temptation and engaging in sexual touch. The penalty can be additional days of enforced abstinence or unpleasant chores that the transgressing partner has to perform. Choose a punishment that is meaningful to both of you to make sure that your no sexual contact on off-sex days prohibition is taken seriously.

> **Sex Rx Rule:** *Attentive Anticipation + Deliberate Deprivation = Greater Gratification. Create deliberate deprivation through prescriptive prohibition against all sexual touch on off-sex days.*

DAY 25

For the next two days, you will practice deliberate deprivation by abstaining from all sexual activity with your partner. You must not make love, kiss, or even touch your partner. The point of this exercise is to demonstrate the power of frustrated desire and the paradoxical nature of longing created through prescribed sexual prohibition. Throughout today, you will also cultivate your longing by visualizing what it would be like to make love to your partner.

1. **Create longing for your partner through directed attention.** Be mindful of your partner throughout the day. Every time you walk by your partner, look at him or her through the prism of your desire. Take time to admire all the features that you find adorable in your partner. Imagine what your partner would look like undressed, what he or she would look like in the throes of sexual ecstasy. Feel the frustration of not being able to have your way with your partner tonight or tomorrow.

2. **Do not hold your partner tonight.** If you usually sleep together, move to the opposite side of the bed; better yet, one of you should relocate to the couch or

guest room for tonight and tomorrow night. Allow yourself to fully feel the annoyance of being told to do this. Fall asleep imagining how exciting it will be to make love to your partner in a couple days. With your eyes closed, try to use all of your senses to invoke the experience of making love to your partner. You can grab an article of clothing from your partner's closet and inhale the familiar aroma of your partner's body, wishing you could hold him or her tight.

DAY 25 SUMMARY

- Create longing for your partner by imagining what it would be to make love to him or her and fretting over the fact that you cannot.
- Drift to sleep imagining making love to your partner and looking forward to it.

DAY 26

Today, you will try another thought-suppression technique to create longing for your partner. Tonight you will pleasure yourself to the thought of making love to your partner while practicing peaking and Kegeling.

1. **Try to suppress all thoughts about having sex with your partner.** First, actively invoke the image of making love to your partner, then tell yourself not to think about it for the next fifteen minutes. The more you try not to think of about making love to your partner, the more preoccupied you should become. Which tech-

nique made you want your partner more: deliberately thinking about having sex with your partner yesterday or actively suppressing the thought about having sex with your partner today? Whichever technique in your opinion fostered greater desire for your partner is the one you should use during your future off-sex days.

2. **Masturbate using Kegeling and peaking.** Make sure your partner is not present or is in the other room while you are engaging in this exercise. You can touch yourself discreetly in the car or in your office. Obviously, use extreme discretion and do not blame us if you get caught! Intensify the desire for your partner by self-pleasuring while fantasizing about him or her. If you can, take a break and send a naughty e-mail or a racy text message to your partner describing how you are playing with yourself to the thought of making love to him or her.

DAY 26 SUMMARY

- Try to suppress all thoughts about your partner by actively attempting not to think of sex with him or her.
- Pleasure yourself while imagining what it would be like to be making love to your partner instead.

CHAPTER 14

Becoming Sexual Soulmates

Although a good physical connection can produce perfectly sat-isfactory orgasms, amazing, time-altering, mind-shattering sex can only happen between sexual soulmates. Sexual soulmates do not view sex as a mere exercise in genital friction; rather, they see it as a metaphysical experience whereby they achieve spiritual union through the merger of their bodies, minds, and souls. To become sexual soulmates is:

- to learn to be mindful by engaging all your senses while making love to your partner;
- to include your partner into your sexual fantasies and make him or her the primary object of your erotic longing;
- to assure your partner's optimal sexual satisfaction by exploring various ways of maximizing his or her erotic pleasure;
- to tune into your partner through eye contact during lovemaking;
- to be sensitive to your partner's emotional needs during lovemaking and during the afterglow;
- and, ideally, to develop an intuitive or psychokinetic understanding of your partner's erotic desires.

Don't forget the importance of mindfulness and inclusion of your partner in your sexual fantasies. And if you haven't already, try eyes-open kissing, which is a prelude to soul-gazing, or open-eyed, lovemaking.

OPEN-EYED LOVEMAKING

Most couples close their eyes when they make love. One way to increase your connectedness with your partner is to have sex with your eyes open so that you can see your partner. But seeing doesn't mean looking at each other's bodies—it involves letting your partner look into your eyes and your soul. Remember the expression, "Eyes are the windows to the soul." This practice of intense eye contact is known as "soul-gazing" in Tantric teaching, and it is supposed to transmit sexual energy. The next time you make love, don't turn off the lights and don't close your eyes. Keep your eyes open throughout the erotic encounter. At the moment of orgasm, look into each other's eyes—you may be surprised by the electrifying power of the connection you experience!

If you find it difficult to orgasm with your eyes open—and many people do—start by kissing your partner with your eyes open. This charges the emotional connection between you, deepens your sexual bond, and brings you a step closer to eyes-open sex. Your mind cannot drift away from intimacy when your eyes are open and focused on your partner's face. If you feel awkward keeping your eyes open for the duration of the kiss, try introducing intermittent pauses for eye contact. If you feel disconnected from your partner while kissing, interrupt the kiss and gaze into his or her eyes, reaching out for a greater emotional bond.

SIMULTANEOUS ORGASMS

Even though we fantasize about climaxing in unison with our partners, in actual fact, a simultaneous orgasm is rare, even for true sexual soulmates. Indeed, it is more common that the woman doesn't reach orgasm at all than that she and her partner orgasm at the same time. This is especially true if the parties are inexperienced or at the beginning of a relationship, when they are still learning one another's responses to various stimuli. Sometimes the attempt or desire for such a result might prevent it, because thinking about it will distract you through the process called "spectatoring"—observing your sexual response instead of enjoying it—and deter your orgasms.

Instead of attempting to synchronize your orgasmic responses with your partner's, take turns, focusing first on one partner's orgasm—generally the woman's—and then on that of the other partner. When a man climaxes, he usually experiences a refractory period when he cannot sustain an erection and has decreased interest in sexual stimulation, whereas a woman can continue with intercourse during her refractory period even after a strong orgasm.

The only practical way to actually experience simultaneous orgasms is if a woman's orgasm triggers the man's orgasm, or vice versa. Although not technically simultaneous, as one immediately follows the other, the overlap provides the feeling of closeness and matching desires that the myth of simultaneous orgasm was striving for. If a man learns to delay his orgasm through peaking or pelvic exercises described earlier (or through mental disengagement), he can remain on the verge of ejaculatory inevitability (close to orgasm) until his partner begins to climax, at which point he can let himself go. Another way to trigger a contemporaneous orgasm is to use a vibrator during intercourse, one that has proven successful at quickly delivering an orgasm to the woman, and to apply that vibration just as the man approaches his own climax.

As you learn to practice eyes-open sex and become more emotionally attuned to your partner, you will be able to feel your partner's escalating level of arousal and recognize signs of his or her impending orgasm. You may even develop psychokinesis or telepathy, whereby you can understand what your partner is thinking or feeling, or relate to her mental state. Some couples report that simultaneous orgasms become commonplace once lovers achieve that level of psychic connection.

Types of Female Orgasm

Traditionally, female orgasms have been classified into *clitoral, vaginal,* and *blended* categories. The clitoral orgasm, often referred to as "hysterical paroxysm," was viewed as inferior by Freud and others until the mid-twentieth century. Such thinking prevailed until Alfred Kinsey's research, published in the book *Sexual Behavior in the Human Female* in 1953, showed that this is the only way a majority of women are able to orgasm. Nowadays, the clitoral/vaginal distinction is considered to be too simplistic, as several different areas that can lead to orgasmic reactions in women have been identified. Many women are unable to identify the exact location of their orgasm, instead reporting "a wave" of pleasurable sensation in the genital area.

Although a majority of women are able to climax during masturbation (usually from clitoral stimulation), many women do not achieve orgasm with a partner. Psychologist and ardent proponent of female autoeroticism, Lonnie Barbach, termed these women "preorgasmic" rather than "anorgasmic." Preorgasmic women frequently go on to achieve orgasms with skillful and attentive partners. For preorgasmic women, mutual masturbation can be an important step to reaching orgasm with a partner. Patience, sensitivity, and sensuality are important for those women who have difficulty reaching orgasms. The first orgasm is usually the most challenging to achieve, although for some women, it occurs by total surprise. For women who are unable to climax otherwise, vibrators may provide sufficient high-intensity stimulation to experience orgasms.

MULTIPLE ORGASMS FOR WOMEN

More than forty-five years ago, the famous scientific team of Masters and Johnson discovered that some women are capable of having more than one orgasm during a sexual session. The research they did showed that men and women have different patterns of arousal. Men take considerably less time to become aroused. Their orgasms are somewhat shorter in duration, and their ejaculation is almost always followed by a sharp drop in arousal. Although a woman takes a longer time to get aroused, her state of arousal does not plummet immediately after orgasm and can continue to remain moderately high after she has climaxed.

Masters and Johnson called this state of continuing arousal "the plateau," and in their research they found some women could enjoy up to twenty successive vaginal orgasms from continuous stimulation. Indeed, later research by the same team discovered a state called *status orgasmus,* or sustained orgasm. In particular, one female subject they examined was able to sustain an orgasm for forty-three seconds with twenty-five separate contractions.

TYPES OF MULTIPLE ORGASMS FOR WOMEN
There are really two types of female multiple orgasms. One is the sequential multiple, during which orgasms are

experienced two to ten minutes apart, with a woman's arousal level declining only to the plateau level and then resuming its climb to a repeat orgasm. The other type is the serial orgasm, during which a woman experiences orgasms one after another without any drop in arousal between them. The sequential multiples are often the product of first attaining clitoral orgasm from oral or manual stimulation and then moving to vaginal intercourse, where further orgasms occur.

In some situations, following up a clitoral orgasm, achieved through lighter pressure by hand or mouth stimulation, with harder stimulation from a sex toy can produce a second clitoral orgasm. On the other hand, serial multiples are almost always vaginal orgasms, often produced by manual G-spot stimulation or during intercourse where the right angle allows the woman to experience the right stimulation for a sufficient time.

GOING FOR THE MULTIPLE WITH VARIED STIMULATION

The key to making your partner experience multiple orgasms appears to be prolonged and varied stimulation. To produce a serial vaginal orgasm through intercourse, you can try to prolong intercourse for ten to thirty minutes at a time and to vary the stimulation you give to your female partner, both in penile angle and in speed and depth of thrust. The easiest way is to let the woman be on top first, where she can move in ways that maximize her pleasure, and allow her to bring herself to climax, or close, in that position. Then, the male partner can take over, and by using faster and harder thrusting, he can sometimes bring her to a second (or more) vaginal orgasm. Varying the positions and types of stimulation, such as adding nipple stimulation, anal fingering, spanking, or using a vibrator at key points, can increase the chance of successive orgasms because the new sensations add to the woman's level of excitement.

Less-taxing sexual positions allow for longer continuous stimulation. Alternating the CAT position, which stimulates the clitoris, with the raised-hip missionary position by placing a pillow under the woman's back, which stimulates the G-spot, produces multiple orgasms in some women. Adding manual or vibrator stimulation, both clitorally and anally, can also enhance and prolong orgasms.

However, even with the best of efforts, not all women will be able to achieve multiple orgasms, and such inability does not make them deficient or inferior lovers. Nevertheless, she will appreciate all the effort you put into maximizing her pleasure. In time, as your sexual compatibility grows and your level of soulmate connection deepens, when you least expect it, she might experience multiple orgasms even if she doesn't think she can.

MULTIPLE ORGASMS FOR MEN

The techniques for achieving male multiple orgasms originate in the Far Eastern sex practices of Tantra and Taoism, discussed in greater depth in the next chapter. The trick to male multiple orgasm is the separation of orgasm and ejaculation. When a man ejaculates, he has little choice but to go into a refractory state, where his arousal is lowered. However, it is possible for a man to experience some of the sensations of orgasm without actually ejaculating; in those cases, he can achieve more than one orgasm during a single sexual session.

THE MANUAL PRESSURE TECHNIQUE

One of these techniques involves pressing on the urethra just before an orgasm to cut off the flow of semen. This is the Jen-Mo technique of the Taoist philosophy, otherwise known as "injaculation," or *coitus saxonus*. This is accomplished by applying finger pressure on the urethra—the tube that runs from the prostate and along the underside of the penis—thus preventing the seminal fluid from traveling through the urethra. The best spot to apply this pressure lies in the perineum just at the base of the penis. When explored with your finger, this area feels like a small indentation in that location. Pressing this point is easy and, with some practice, the man can do it without his partner even noticing.

If he is in the missionary position, all he needs to do is to reach back with his hand, locate the indentation between his anus and scrotum, and apply firm pressure right before he feels an oncoming orgasm. His female partner can do this for him, as well.

By applying this urethral pressure, some men are able to stop and restart ejaculation. If the pressure is sufficiently hard and prolonged, you will injaculate—that is, ejaculate into the bladder if the pressure is closer to the scrotum or into the bloodstream if the pressure is closer to the prostate gland. During injaculation, you still experience orgasm but continue to maintain your erection. It is harmless so long as it is not done violently or too often. Some men report longer orgasms using this technique, whereas others claim it does not work for them.

PC MUSCLE CONTRACTION TECHNIQUE

Another technique used to achieve multiple orgasms involves PC muscle control achieved through Kegeling (an important element of this program). With practice, you can learn to shut off your seminal flow by contracting this muscle after you feel the upcoming orgasm but before the ejaculatory point of no return (termed "ejaculatory inevitability").

The trick is to be able to identify the beginning of the orgasm phase, when the seminal fluid (or "precum," in lay terms) appears and muscular rigidity begins to set in right before the release of tension. At the point of impending orgasm and before the point of no return, the man must contract the pelvic muscle with sufficient pressure to be able to stop the ejaculation. A small amount of sperm might still seep out, but you should still be very aroused and able to continue penile stimulation. The best way to learn this is by using peaking (which we have included in the exercises throughout the book) during masturbatory practices, where you can pace yourself and learn to identify the stages of your sexual response cycle.

CONNECTING AFTERWARD

One of the most frequent complaints women have about men is their lack of desire to engage in afterplay. Many men have an irresistible postejaculatory urge to turn over and snore, and this urge has a biological basis. The blood rush after climax depletes the muscles of energy-producing glycogen, leaving men feeling physically drained. According to one study, 80 percent of men said they felt more relaxed and were able to drift off without any problems after making love, compared with 46 percent of women. The survey also found that 48 percent of men had actually fallen asleep during the act itself, compared to a mere 11 percent of women who admitted being guilty of this. Women, on the other hand, are programmed to seek attachment and intimacy after sex. The reason women have a greater desire to cuddle after sex is that women's bodies put out 50 percent more oxytocin than men's bodies, the warm and fuzzy cuddle hormone. And women usually need more of that feeling of closeness and bonding, as their sex drive is more closely linked to their emotional needs. Her way of expressing appreciation for good sex is through affection; she wants to feel that he appreciates her efforts as well.

These differences can cause unintentional hurt between couples. As one female client said, "It always hurts my feelings when my husband completely spaces out after he has his orgasm. It's like a light goes out in his head, and he is no longer interested in paying any attention to me." Communication can help clear up these misunderstandings; however, it also helps if the male partner holds and cuddles with the female partner afterwards, at least for a little while. Remember, the five A's of intimacy: attention, affection, appreciation, affirmation, and adoration? Give her at least one or a bit of each after making love to her. Tell her how much you enjoyed making love to her, what a great lover she is, how wonderful it felt to be inside her, and how thankful you are to have her in your life. *Then* tell her you need a nap. Being a sexual soulmate requires sensitivity to your partner's sexual and emotional needs.

> **Sex Rx Rule:** *Sexual soulmates view sex as a merger of their minds, bodies, and souls, and they seek to maximize each other's erotic enjoyment and to fulfill one another's sexual and emotional needs.*

DAY 27

Because the last two days were your off-sex days, the next several days are all-sex days. If you practiced the exercises we assigned during the last two days, you should be replete with longing and lust for your partner. Now we want you to carve out time for prolonged, passionate lovemaking tonight. Today, you will work on connecting with each other on a deeper, more soulful level and also sexually exploring each other in ways you have not done before, seeking to discover ways of maximizing each other's pleasure.

1. **Before making love, connect on a soulful level by getting away from banal banter to discuss loftier**

topics. Research shows that discussing loftier topics such as philosophy, religion, existential meaning, global history, and politics makes couples feel much happier and more connected than regular small talk. So as much as you may be tempted to succumb to daily gossip about your coworkers and celebrities, such talk will not bring you closer to your partner.

Today, probe your partner's mind with existential questions such as "How do you envision us in twenty years?" "What kind of world do you think our children will inhabit?" "How do you define love?" "What would you tell me if you knew that the world would end in a few days in massive apocalypse?" "What are the five things you want to do before you die?" "Do you think being loved makes one immortal?"

2. **Make eyes-open love tonight.** Don't dim the lights in the room and try to keep your eyes open throughout the entire erotic encounter with your partner. If you feel like you are staring, soften the gaze. You can avert your eyes occasionally, but try to look into each other's eyes when the orgasm is approaching. Orgasm is a vulnerable moment, and our faces betray many emotions at the moment of climax. Seek to establish a soulful connection with your partner by seeing yourself, your past, and your future together in your partner's eyes. This soul-gazing experience may feel awkward at first, but it is an important step toward becoming sexual soulmates.

3. **Experiment to see if she can have multiple clitoral orgasms tonight.** Begin with very slow and gentle stimulation of her clitoris with your fingers and tongue. Most women will orgasm when clitoral stimulation is in the right place and provided for a sufficiently long time. Do not intensify the stimulation—aim to bring

her to an orgasm from the lightest possible touch of your fingers and tongue.

After her first orgasm, continue the stimulation but make it very light for a few minutes. Then depending on your partner's feedback, see how she feels when you introduce more intense clitoral stimulation with your fingers or a vibrator. At this point you can add light vaginal and anal fingering, depending on her response. Do not put pressure on yourself to bring her to a second climax—simply observe if it can happen by increasing the amount and type of stimulation. Many women are able to have another contemporaneously close clitoral orgasm if the first one was produced through light stimulation, followed by more intense stimulation with a vibrator.

4. **Connect in the afterglow of the orgasm for at least fifteen minutes.** Do not rush to wash or clean up—hold the partner who has climaxed last. Feel the mind-bending, time-altering quality of amazing sex. Orgasm triggers oxytocin release, that warm, bonding, trust-promoting hormone we have discussed before, making it the perfect time to connect with each other. Do not turn away, fall asleep, look at the clock, turn on the TV, or begin talking about mundane things.

Continue to touch, kiss, and caress each other prolonging the moment of the afterglow as you imagine that time stands still. If you do something, try doing it in slow motion. Visualize the intensity of sexual experience like a big wave that has picked you up and thrown you on an uninhabited island, and you are lying on the warm sand, feeling the eternity in the tidal whispering of the ocean. You have nowhere to go and nothing to do, except merge with each other. Inquire what each of you would do, alone and together, on this deserted island meant for just you two.

DAY 27 SUMMARY

- Strip daily layers of psychic defenses by engaging in deep, soulful talk about lofty topics.
- Engage in the soul-gazing technique of eyes-open sex and attempt to lock your gaze with that of your partner at the moment of orgasm.
- Experiment to see if your female partner can have more than one clitoral orgasm by introducing different types of oral and manual stimulation and increasing its intensity after the first orgasm.
- Use the afterglow time to connect on a deep, soulful level. Visualize lying on the beach of a deserted island, holding each other, where time stands still. Share your emotions evoked by that image.

DAY 28

Today you will continue to deepen your connection as sexual soulmates by working on enhancing your physical as well as your mental connection with your partner.

1. **Try hypnotic self-suggestions to enhance your passionate bonding.** Use the visualization exercises described in Chapter 3 to create an alternate world with the two of you enjoying a satisfying, rewarding relationship and amazing sex life. See yourself and your partner as happy, relaxed, and committed people. Feel

the love between you. Create the perfect picture. Then relax and let the picture disappear.

2. **Prolong intercourse for as long as possible.** See if either or both of you can experience multiple orgasms. Try the CAT technique, where the male partner is riding higher in the saddle during the missionary position, providing direct clitoral contact for the woman with his pubic bone. Alternate it with the modified missionary, where her legs are bent all the way up to her chin for maximizing G-spot stimulation. Try squeezing your PC muscle by Kegeling (which you have been practicing) to see if such contraction triggers or intensifies your orgasm or that of your partner. The male partner can try to identify when he is approaching the point of no return and stop the ejaculation by either contracting his PC muscle or pressing on the perineum as described earlier.

3. **See if you can achieve simultaneous or contemporaneous orgasms by synchronizing your arousal and then letting one partner's orgasm trigger the other's.** Try to guess your partner's level of arousal by gazing into his eyes, listening to his breathing, feeling the escalating warmth of his body. Get your partner's feedback by asking her to lead you through the arousal phase by verbalizing her level of arousal, such as "I am almost there. I feel like I need another minute/a few more strokes to get there." But do not put any pressure on yourself to achieve the synchronicity—think of it as a playful sexploration to expand your sexual repertoire and enhance your compatibility.

4. **Connect during the afterglow for at least twenty minutes.** This time, try a spooning position, where one partner completely envelops the other with his or her limbs. Hold your partner's arms and hands with

yours. Do you feel completely safe and protected in this position? Mentally connect the sensation of safety and security with the thought, "My partner gives me security and safety." Then try a cradling position, where you lay your head on your partner's chest and he or she cradles it and strokes your hair. Listen to your partner's heartbeat. Do you feel loved and adored in this position? Mentally connect the sensation of being loved with the affirmative thought, "My partner loves and adores me."

DAY 28 SUMMARY

- Use hypnotic self-suggestions to increase your emotional bond with your partner.
- Prolong intercourse as long as possible, exploring potential multiple orgasms.
- See if you can have a simultaneous orgasm by synchronizing your sensations and letting one partner's orgasm trigger the other's.
- Connect during afterglow physically through spooning and cradling, while you mentally link the sensation of being protected and loved with the affirmation that it is indeed so.

Bonus for Her: Intensify His Orgasm

The *coitus a la Florentine* technique can be used to speed up and intensify male orgasm. This is accomplished by holding the man's penile skin forcibly back at the root of the penis with your finger and thumb and keeping it stretched all the time, using an up-and-down stroke. If the right tension is achieved, this technique speeds up ejaculation and boosts the sensation of the male orgasm.

Insight for Him and Her

Some days your partner fakes an orgasm. Indeed, some research shows that up to 80 percent of women do it half of the time. Unfortunately, faking gives him a false impression of the efficacy of his sexual technique, perhaps preventing him from improving it. One of the most common reasons women fake it is response anxiety—the desire to respond in a way their partner expects them to. Some women are afraid they are taking too long or feel rushed by their partner. That is why it is paramount for men to express their patience and enjoyment of performing oral sex or intercourse on their woman for as long as it takes. Becoming sexual soulmates will make you more attuned to your partner's mood and timing, and will eliminate much of the response anxiety.

Men also on occasion fake orgasms. Men may do it for the same reason as women: They are tired or feel distant, or they don't want to offend their partner. Some do it because they are on medication that delays ejaculation, and others do it to mask the loss of an erection. If you suspect your partner is faking it, it is best not to confront him or her directly to avoid embarrassing your partner. Instead, try varying your lovemaking technique, observe your partner's reaction, and solicit his or her feedback.

CHAPTER 15

Transcending the Physical

On the surface there seems to be little in common between spirituality and sexuality. Yet universally, in every language and culture, humans summon deity when they are in the throes of passion, crying out "Oh, my God!" "God, please don't stop!" Both sexuality and spirituality are transcendental experiences in that they connect us with each other and elevate us above our mundane existence, altering our sense of time and space. Both experiences are enhanced through ritual accoutrements such as candles, music, and incense. In Maslow's definition, both religious and sexual ecstasy are peak experiences.

What is particularly fascinating is that both are processed primarily in the right side of the brain, in the right temporal lobe and prefrontal cortex. Because the right hemisphere is involved in processing music and rhythm, you can use mystical music to activate the right hemisphere and create a more lofty lovemaking atmosphere. The right hemisphere also mitigates our anxieties and worries, so creating relaxation rituals that involve bathing, massage, meditation, and candlelight will calm your nervous brain and prime you for spiritual sex.

SPIRITUAL SEX IN ANCIENT SCHOOLS OF TANTRA AND KABBALAH

Sex, as a spiritual act that involves the exchange of energy forces, has been described in many religions. The best-known of these are Tantra and Kabbalah. Both Tantra and Kabbalah believe in the life-affirming libidinal energy that pulses through the universe and teach that we can tap into and transmit this energy during soulful sex. Both traditions view sex as a sacred ritual that elevates us above our mundane experiences by expanding our consciousness and connecting us with the great cosmic life force. Sex becomes an act of worship, a mystical journey, a spiritual ecstasy.

TANTRA

The best-known of spiritual sexual practices is Tantra, which means "woven together" in Sanskrit. Tantra is most commonly mentioned in reference to Hindu yogic practices, but it has been applied to the sexual practices of many other Eastern religions, including Tibetan Buddhism and Taoism. Tantric practices are speculated to be more than 4,000 years old.

The sexual aspect of ancient Tantra was a small part of the larger quest for connecting with the creator. It required a male follower to spend years preparing for an enlightening evening of spiritual love with a Tantra goddess, or sacred temple prostitute. This was a highly anticipated and ritualized ceremony during which he would carnally entwine with a woman he had never seen before, a woman who was a symbolic representation of the immortal feminine principle. The rigorous process of preparation for this union with the cosmic womb was undertaken under the guidance of a guru who had himself attained such enlightenment. The preparation included learning the mechanics of total ejaculatory self-control. On a chosen night, the worshipper was led into the chamber of devotional delight, where he would unite with the sexual temple priestess, entering the womb of the universe through her. They would remain entwined for hours in a deep state of communion, exploring the cosmic consciousness. Eventually the worshipper would experience a cosmically charged internal orgasm (or injacula-tion) that would bring him permanent divine enlightenment.

Over the centuries Tantric practices have become synony-mous with accessing divinity through sexuality. Unlike Western sexuality, which is goal-oriented—the goal being an orgasm—Tantric sexuality is means-oriented. It focuses on connection and on harnessing emotions as opposed to mere procure-ment of pleasure. By living in a constant state of preorgasm and prolonging sex as long as possible, Tantric practitioners seek to harness the erotic energy and reach expansion of con-sciousness. According to Tantric teachings, sexual energy, called *kundalini*, has healing properties and can cure both body and spirit through erotic envelopment and restoration of the life force. Sex is not merely about penetration, but about unity of the bodies, the rubbing and merger of which generate both heat and enlightenment.

KABBALAH

Mystical Jewish teachings, called Kabbalah, also view sex as a tool for expanding consciousness. The literal meaning of the word *kabbalah* is "to receive," and its practitioners seek to turn everyday experiences into receptacles of the divine. In the Kabbalistic view, the divine resides in every fiber of material existence and God can be found everywhere. In this perspec-tive, the body is just as holy as the soul.

God carries both male and female energy; the feminine part of God created the universe from the cosmic womb, whereas the male part of God rewards the good and punishes the bad. Sex unifies a man and a woman and symbolizes the blending of two divine energies. Thus sex is sacred because it involves the union of the opposites, merging our sexual energy, and becoming one with the universal energy. Sex is the most profound and potent spiritual conduit, and our intense moments of sexual intimacy reverberate through the cosmos, sending waves of loving energy like ripples from a stone fallen in the cosmic water.

KAREZZA AS A SPIRITUAL INTERCOURSE

Karezza (or *coitus reservatus*) is a more recent form of spiritual sex not connected to any religious school of thought. It is a gentle, spiritual form of intercourse in which orgasm ideally does not occur in either partner while making love. The term comes from the Italian word *carezza,* meaning "caress," and it was coined by Alice Bunker Stockham, MD, at the end of the nineteenth century. Stockham's work was initially inspired by the work of John Humphrey Noyes, who developed a concept of so-called male continence to teach men to avoid ejaculation when conception was not desired. Stockham took this concept further by proposing that both males and females would benefit from passing up orgasm.

Stockham believed that each sex act should be preceded by some form of spiritual dedication, such as writing love letters, scheduling dates, spending at least an hour away from the children, lighting candles, or sharing a glass of wine. She also suggested keeping separate bedrooms so that each sex act was deliberate and not just a prelude to going to sleep. Both males and females should try to avoid orgasm for as long as possible until it naturally results from the overflow of stimulation, as an outcome of bodily and spiritual rapture.

Other than the aforementioned principles, there are no techniques involved in the practice of Karezza. It is about learning to experience each other without expectations, pressures, or goals. In this way each couple creates its own experiential version of Karezza.

Although Karezza is premised on being engaged in intercourse, the emphasis is on expressing affection and mutual adoration while avoiding performance pressures and striving to achieve an orgasm. Many Karezza practitioners use abdominal breathing (discussed in the first part of this book) throughout the lovemaking session to achieve and maintain a deeply relaxed state.

Whereas Tantra and Kabbalah utilize prolonged intercourse as an act of worship with the goal of uniting with universal life force, Karezza is entirely goal-free. Unlike Tantric sex positions (many of which are quite acrobatic and require athletic effort), sexual positions during Karezza should be as comfortable as possible and require little or no effort. A male partner doesn't have to remain hard the entire time. Erections can rise and fall with no performance pressure at all, and some couples even fall asleep in this relaxed interconnected state. Unlike Tantra, Karezza requires no specialized techniques or visualizations of energy and purportedly leads to the same deeply satisfying bonding by triggering the relaxation response through deep breathing and releasing copious amounts of our favorite hormone, oxytocin. Its only goal is to bring the partners closer together. By striving for a genuine, warm, and lasting human bond instead of a momentary release of sexual tension, it elevates sex from the mundane to the lofty.

SELECTING YOUR OWN SACRED SEXUALITY SCRIPT

The premise of all spiritual sexual premises is the same: to use sexual union not as a means for releasing sexual tension, but as a conduit for transcendence and connection with the universe. Seeking sexual spirituality is a worthy cause as studies show that spiritual people have better marriages, live longer, deal better with stress, and are happier and healthier. And you don't have to be religious to be spiritual. You simply need to believe that something outside the mere physicality of your being exists and to feel your transcendental nature through the blissful fusion of your souls. Spiritual sex can become your quest as a couple for experiencing the universal energy of life and seeking symbolic immortality through the sacred union of your souls.

Sex Rx Rule: *Soulful Connection + Slow, Sensuous Lovemaking = Spiritual Sex*

DAY 29

Today, you will attempt to expand your sexual consciousness by exploring spiritual dimensions through the practices of ancient schools of spiritual sexuality. Although some of these practices may seem odd to you, do not discount the time-proven wisdom of these spiritual techniques without practicing them a few times.

1. **Try the kundalini meditation ritual, purported to release sexual energy.** This form of meditation involves chanting five primal sounds: saa, taa, naa, maa, and aa, while consecutively touching your thumbs to fingers two, three, four, and five. Repeat the sounds and finger touching for two minutes out loud, two minutes whispering, four minutes silently, two minutes whispering, and two minutes out loud.

   In a research study, meditation subjects reported an increase in sexual desire following practice of this ritual.

2. **Now try an energizing Tantric breath technique, also from the kundalini tradition, called the Breath of Fire, which is designed to ignite your sexual fires.** Sit up straight facing your partner and hold hands.

Look at each other and begin panting fast and very hard, making a hissing sound as you inhale and exhale, continuing for about ten to fifteen seconds, attempting to synchronize your voices. Feel your breaths connect and spark the desire within you.

3. **Tonight, try the ancient practice of one-night-with-a-goddess-reincarnate.** One of you should be designated as the sacred temple goddess or god—there is no reason why you should perpetuate gender stereotypes here. The designated "deity" should retreat into the bedroom—the temple—and dress in a divine manner. The temple can be enhanced with Tantric accoutrements such as sandalwood or musk incense. At a designated time, the worshipper enters the temple and kneels before the goddess or god. Then the deity guides the worshipper on the transcendental journey by instructing the worshipper to get undressed and enter the sacred tunnel of divine energy (or be impaled on the sacred tunnel). Practice slow, sensuous Tantric lovemaking with your god or goddess. Remember, according to the Tantric doctrine, such spiritual sex can lead to multiple orgasms, but a man needs to practice semen retention by either pressing his perineum or contracting his PC muscle, resulting in either a dry orgasm or injaculation.

DAY 29 SUMMARY

- Try the sexual energy–releasing meditation ritual by chanting primal sounds while touching your fingers.
- Try the sexual energy–igniting breathing ritual by panting fast together in synchronicity.

- Plan an evening of worshipping your sacred temple goddess or god. Make slow Tantric love to your deity, as a conduit to the universal erotic energy.

DAY 30

Today you will finish our program while continuing your soul-searching spiritual journey. Ultimately you'll decide as a couple which of the suggestions and techniques will become a part of your new and ever-changing sexual script.

1. **Try a sort of Tantric astral projection technique to learn nonphysical connection.** Astral projection is a Tantric concept similar to the Western concept of telepathy or psychokinesis, whereby you are able to read your partner's thoughts and transmit energy between you. Sit across from your partner with your eyes closed. Now visualize sending a ball of hot energy across to your partner, and imagine him or her reciprocating. Try to guess what your partner is thinking and feeling by attuning yourself to your partner's energy field.

2. **Give a prayer to the Eros Deity.** This is not a religious prayer; rather it is your attempt to feel more connected to each other and to the erotic energy around you by expressing your gratitude and longing for it (although if you are religious, feel free to modify it in accordance with your beliefs). Have fun composing this prayer and the ritual that will go along with it. You can surround your bed with candles or incense and play mystical music.

    Our prayer goes something like this: "Oh, Eros and Venus, thank you for the everlasting longing you installed in our hearts for each other. Please lead us into temptation to explore each other's erotic depths and to experience the rare and sheer bliss of using our sexual union for connecting with the universal energy, transcending time and space, and finding our heaven on earth."

3. **Engage in Karezza by practicing gentle, nonorgasmic intercourse.** Begin by eliminating distractions and spending some time talking, kissing, and cuddling. Then assume a comfortable sexual position—side-by-side positions are ideal for Karezza as they involve minimal friction. Gaze into each other's eyes and breathe deeply, aiming for total relaxation. If you feel orgasm approaching, slow down until the desire subsides. Take lots of long, restful pauses.

   Neither one of you should climax, for as long as possible. Eventually you should both feel the flowing state of continuous orgasm, a peculiar state of psychedelic perception of timelessness, although it may take a few days or weeks of practicing Karezza regularly to get there. Put the attainment of orgasm out of your mind and instead focus on experiencing mutual pleasure and creating a deep, loving connection with your partner.

DAY 30 SUMMARY

- Try the astral projection or telepathy technique, whereby you project energy toward your partner and tune in to his or her thoughts and feelings.
- Make up an erotic deity prayer through which you express your gratitude for your erotic union.
- Try Karezza, a slow, effortless, and completely pressure-free intercourse aimed at passing up orgasms and instead focusing on creating a deep, lasting bond and connection.

Insight for Him and Her

Some men are unable to master the orgasm-delaying techniques required for spiritual sex no matter how hard they practice them. Latest research shows that it is because they are genetically predisposed to early ejaculation and, in some, the condition may be intractable. Medication can be helpful in these cases. Evidence shows that some men with rapid ejaculation respond well to SSRI inhibitor drugs, such as Zoloft and Prozac. Some practitioners report 80 percent improvement in cases of early ejaculation with the use of Paxil, but the drug must continue to be used in order to ensure longer latency of orgasm. Because treatments for rapid ejaculation and other sexual concerns are highly individualized, men or couples concerned about it should seek the help of a physician or trained sex therapist.

Afterword

Congratulations! You've completed our Sex Rx Program, a challenging and intensive program requiring commitment, determination, an open mind, focus, and lots of time and emotional labor. Now you may want to go back and briefly look over the summaries at the end of each chapter to decide which ideas and practices you have enjoyed as a couple and which ones you want to continue practicing.

To solidify your new erotically charged practices into habits, you need to consistently practice them for at least twenty-one days, as that's about the length of time it takes for a ritual to become habitual. Don't forget about engaging in physical exercise together, practicing Kegeling, adding aphrodisiacs, setting date nights, surprise nights, off-sex nights and all-sex nights, practicing the 5 C's, expressing the 3 G's and 5 A's, flirting, mirroring, and seducing your partner, drawing from your Jar of Desires, adding items to your Sexual Menu and His and Her Pleasure Manual, experimenting with new sounds and smells, trying new techniques and positions, soul-gazing through eyes-open sex, meditating together, and seeking symbolic immortality through soulful sexual union.

Don't panic if you forget to do any of the above, because the total impact of this program is greater than the sum of its parts. By undertaking this journey together, you have already become better lovers and partners because you have improved your chemistry, commitment, compatibility, communication, and cooperation. The suggestions we offered are merely tools for putting together the blueprint of your personal Happily Ever After, which you are now ready to assemble.

> **Sex Rx Rule:** *Continue to practice your favorite erotic exercises from this book for at least twenty-one days for the ritual to become habitual.*

You may feel that the information in this book is overwhelming and a bit intimidating. Yet we can summarize it for you in a few sentences. Make your sexual health and time with your partner priorities. Be grateful and let go of grudges. Take time to compliment and appreciate each other. Be inventive and playful, and a bit naughty. If you want truly great sex, seek to merge your bodies, minds, and souls.

Variety is the spice of sex, and by experimenting and constant expanding your sexual horizons, you will stave off boredom and stagnation. By giving sex priority, cultivating intimacy, introducing novelty, allowing for some naughtiness, and seeing the loftiness of your sexual union, you'll not only keep the flame of your passion alive, but you'll find it burns at an intensity you never thought possible.

Sex Resources

RECOMMENDED NONFICTION

Amen, Daniel G. *Sex on the Brain: 12 Lessons to Enhance Your Love Life*. New York, NY: Three Rivers Press, a division of Random House Inc., 2007.

Bader, Michael J. *Arousal: The Secret Logic of Sexual Fantasies*. New York, NY: Thomas Dunne Books, an imprint of St. Martin's Press, 2002.

Baer, Greg. *Real Love: The Truth about Finding Unconditional Love and Fulfilling Relationships*. New York, NY: Gotham Books, a division of Putnam Penguin Inc., 2003.

Bagarozzi, Dennis A. *Enhancing Intimacy in Marriage: A Clinician's Guide*. Ann Arbor, MI: Sheridan Books, 2001.

Boteach, Shmuley. *The Kosher Sutra: 8 Sacred Secrets for Reigniting Desire and Restoring Passion for Life*. New York, NY: HarperCollins, 2009.

Bouchez, Collette. *The V Zone: A Woman's Guide to Intimate Health Care*. New York, NY: Fireside Publishing, 2001.

Cane, William. *The Art of Kissing*. New York, NY: St. Martin's Press, 1995.

Comfort, Alex. *The Joy of Sex*. New York, NY: Octopus Publishing Group Ltd., 2002.

Fisher, Helen. *Anatomy of Love: A Natural History of Mating, Marriage, and Why We Stray*. New York, NY: Random House, 1992.

Fisher, Helen E. *Why We Love: The Nature and Chemistry of Romantic Love*. New York, NY: Henry Holt and Company, 2004.

Hartley, Nina. *Nina Hartley's Guide to Total Sex*. New York, NY: Penguin Group, 2006.

Heiman, Julia; LoPiccolo, Joseph; and Palladini, David. *Becoming Orgasmic: A Sexual and Personal Growth Program for Women* (2nd ed.) Englewood Cliffs, NJ: Prentice Hall, 1998.

Kerner, Ian. *Sex Detox: Recharge Desire. Revitalize Intimacy. Rejuvenate Your Love Life*. New York, NY: HarperCollins, 2008.

Leiblum, Sandra, and Sachs, Judith. *Getting the Sex You Want: A Woman's Guide to Becoming Proud, Passionate, and Pleased in Bed*. Lincoln, NE: ASJA Press, an imprint of iUniverse Inc., 2002.

Love, Patricia. *The Truth about Love: The Highs, the Lows, and How You Can Make It Last Forever*. New York, NY: Fireside, 2001.

Mitchell, Stephen A. *Can Love Last? The Fate of Romantic Love Over Time*. New York, NY: W. W. Norton & Company, 2002.

Morin, Jack. *The Erotic Mind: Unlocking the Inner Sources of Passion and Fulfillment*. New York, NY: HarperCollins, 1995.

Rosen, Raymond C., and Leiblum, Sandra. *Erectile Disorders: Assessment and Treatment*. New York, NY: The Guilford Press, 1992.

Royalle, Candida. *How to Tell a Naked Man What to Do: Sex Advice from a Woman Who Knows*. New York, NY: Fireside, 2004.

Schnarch, David. *Passionate Marriage: Keeping Love and Intimacy Alive in Committed Relationships*. New York, NY: W. W. Norton & Company, 1997.

Sprinkle, Annie. *Dr. Sprinkle's Spectacular Sex: Make Over Your Love Life with One of the World's Great Sex Experts*. New York, NY: Jeremy Tarcher/Penguin, 2005.

Taylor, John Maxwell. *Eros Ascending: The Life-Transforming Power of Sacred Sexuality*. Berkeley, CA: North Atlantic Books, 2009.

Warren, John, and Warren, Libby. *The Loving Dominant*. Oakland, CA: Greenery Press, 2008.

RECOMMENDED EROTIC FICTION

Barbach, Lonnie Garfield. *Pleasures: Women Write Erotica*. New York, NY: Perennial Library, 1985.

Corn, Laura. *101 Nights of Grrreat Sex: Secret Sealed Seductions for Fun-Loving Couples*. New York, NY: Park Avenue Publishers, 2000.

Finz, Iris, and Finz, Steven. *Whispered Secrets: The Couple's Guide to Erotic Fantasy*. New York, NY: Signet, 1990.

Friday, Nancy. *Forbidden Flowers: More Women's Sexual Fantasies*. New York, NY: Pocket Books, 1975.

_____. *My Secret Garden: Women's Sexual Fantasies*. New York, NY: Pocket Books, 2003.

_____. *Women on Top*. New York, NY: Pocket Books, 1991.

Jakubowski, Maxim, ed. *The Mammoth Book of Best New Erotica*. Volume 3. Running Press, 2004.

Kronhausen, Phyllis, and Kronhausen, Eberhard. *Erotic Fantasies: A Study of Sexual Imagination*. New York, NY: Grove Press, 1969.

RECOMMENDED EROTIC MAINSTREAM FILMS (R AND NC-17)

Bad Timing: A Sensual Obsession (1980, Dir. Alex Linden). Features graphic sex and other kinks.

Basic Instinct (1992, Dir. Paul Verhoeven). Features exhibitionism/voyeurism and BDSM.

Bitter Moon (1992, Dir. Roman Polanski). Features role-play and BDSM.

Body Heat (1981, Dir. Lawrence Kasdan). Features oral play.

The Brown Bunny (2003, Dir. Vincent Gallo). Features oral play.

Bull Durham (1988, Dir. Ron Shelton). Features passionate intercourse.

Caligula (1980, Dir. Tinto Brass, Bob Guccione, and Giancarlo Lui). Features BDSM, anal, and many fetishes.

Carrie (1976, Dir. Brian De Palma). Features oral play.

Chocolat (2000, Dir. Lasse Hallstrom). Features food play.

Cruel Intentions (1999, Dir. Roger Kumble). Features anal play.

Dangerous Liaisons (1988, Dir. Stephen Frears). Features BDSM.

Do the Right Thing (1989, Dir. Spike Lee). Features ice play.

The Double Life of Veronique (1991, Dir. Krzysztof Kieslowski). Features multiple partners.

Emmanuelle (1974, Dir. Just Jaeckin). Features multiple partners.

Eyes Wide Shut (1999, Dir. Stanley Kubrick). Features exhibitionism/voyeurism.

The Hunger (1983, Dir. Tony Scott). Features oral play and BDSM.

In the Realm of the Senses (1977, Dir. Nagisa Oshima). Features BDSM.

Last Tango in Paris (1972, Dir. Bernardo Bertolucci). Features anal play.

Like Water for Chocolate (1992, Dir. Alfonso Arau). Features food play.

Myra Breckinridge (1970, Dir. Michael Sarne). Features anal and oral play.

9½ Weeks (1986, Dir. Adrian Lyne). Features role-play and BDSM.

The Piano (1993, Dir. Jane Campion). Features oral play, voyeurism, and BDSM.

Sex and Lucia (2001, Dir. Julio Medem). Features multiple partners.

Swept Away (1975, Dir. Lina Wertmuller). Features BDSM elements.

Story of O (1975, Dir. Just Jaeckin). Features BDSM.

Tampopo (1987, Dir. Juzo Itami). Features food play.

Tie Me Up! Tie Me Down! (1990, Dir. Pedro Almodovar). Features BDSM.

Tom Jones (1963, Dir. Tony Richardson). Features food play.

The Unbearable Lightness of Being (1988, Dir. Philip Kaufman). Features multiple partners.

Wild Things (1998, Dir. John McNaughton). Features multiple partners.

Y Tu Mama Tambien (2001, Dir. Alfonso Cuaron). Features multiple partners.

RECOMMENDED ADULT AND PORN FILMS (X-RATED)

Bobby Sox

Bridal Shower

Deep Throat

The Devil in Miss Jones

The Dinner Party

Edge Play

Every Woman Has a Fantasy

The Opening of Misty Beethoven

Zazel: The Scent of Love

FILMS BY THE FOLLOWING PRODUCERS:

- **Andrew Blake:** features beautiful people; dreamy, slow-action shots in exotic locales; emphasis on lesbian erotica.
- **Veronica Hart:** features female-sensitive plot lines, strong women, hard and explicit sex.
- **Nina Hartley:** features porn star and writer Nina and her friends; emphasis on educational, casual, intimate, how-to approach.
- **Michael Ninn:** features beautiful people and opulent locations; fast-paced, intense, music-video style cinematography, with lots of fetish sex.
- **Candida Royalle:** female-sensitive plot lines, natural-looking actresses, story lines with real characters and issues.

Index

About the Authors

John and Victoria met fifteen years ago in a club outside Washington, DC, called quite prophetically, Sesto Senso, which means "sixth sense" in Italian. Barely a week later, they moved in together, full of hope and promise of "happily thereafter." Their journey turned out to be a bumpy ride with many detours and derailments along the way, not least because of their different personalities and values.

Outgoing and laid-back John was born in Barcelona, Spain, a warm and sunny country with a culture that emphasized the importance of time with family and friends, of siestas and fiestas. Intense and driven Victoria grew up in Kiev, Ukraine, an austere place ruled by the Soviets who stressed hard work, societal service, and self-sacrifice, a land of *subbotniks*, or voluntary unpaid work on Saturdays.

As with other couples, their passion for each other was affected by lack of money, career dissatisfaction, intrusive in-laws, meddling siblings, treacherous friends, and personal demons created by childhood legacies and coming-of-age experiences.

When Victoria finished her law degree, she decided she abhorred the practice of law and undertook a long and arduous road to complete her PhD in clinical psychology. John decided he no longer wanted to practice massage therapy and embarked upon finding his passion, eventually enrolling in a master's degree program in marriage and family therapy.

As they studied ways of helping others, they made the mistakes other couples often do, including putting passion at the bottom of their to-do list. This book was born out of not only their clinical experience but also their quest to keep their passion alive through the years. Their hope is that you, like they, will learn to put your best effort into not only resparking the sexual desire you once had for each other, but taking it to the higher level of erotically charged living, one you never thought was possible.